Winning the NFL Way

Mike Sherman

Winning
the NFL Way

LEADERSHIP LESSONS FROM
FOOTBALL'S TOP HEAD COACHES

Bob LaMonte

with Robert L. Shook

HarperBusiness
An Imprint of HarperCollinsPublishers

HarperCollins books may be purchased for educational, business, or sales promotional use. For information, please write: Special Markets Department, HarperCollins Publishers Inc., 10 East 53rd Street, New York, NY 10022.

FIRST EDITION

Designed by Richard Oriolo

Printed on acid-free paper

Library of Congress Cataloging-in-Publication Data has been applied for.

ISBN 0-06-073883-9

04 05 06 07 08 WBC/RRD 10 9 8 7 6 5 4 3 2 1

To Lynn
Thank you for completing my life.

Acknowledgments

First and foremost, we are indebted to the five head coaches featured in this book. Thank you Andy, John, Jon, Mike, and Mike for giving us the time to conduct lengthy interviews with you during our visits at your summer camps prior to the start of the 2003 season. Knowing you work long hours during the preseason, we deeply appreciate your giving us the time to share your insight on leadership with us. Obviously, without your input, this book could not have been written.

We are also grateful to the following people with the Carolina Panthers, Green Bay Packers, Philadelphia Eagles, Seattle Seahawks, and Tampa Bay Buccaneers organizations: Mark Arteaga, Derek Boyko, Susan Broberg, Butch Buchanico, Rick Burkholder, Brad Childress, Garrett Giemont, Gil Haskell, Erik Kennedy, Bill Nayes, Linda O'Hora, Gary Reynolds, Leslie Scarandino, Sal Sunseri, Arleatta Williams, and Carol Wilson. We thank each of you for your valuable contributions to this book.

A special thank-you goes to Misti Candreva, Carole Terrell, and Marlys Zusy, three special women at Professional Sports Representation, Inc. You're simply the best! We also thank Debbie Watts, who did a terrific job transcribing our recorded interviews. Hats off to our literary agent, Basil Kane. Basil's belief and support early on in this project reinforced our belief that we were on to something very special. It has been a pleasure to work with Mauro DiPreta, our editor at HarperCollins, a real professional and a super guy. The same goes for Mauro's assistant, Joelle Yudin, another star at HarperCollins.

Like the five head coaches featured in this book, we are blessed to have a great group of people on our team. As we learned during the writing of this book on leadership, nobody does it alone.

Contents

Introduction: It's Not About the X's and O's—
It's About the CEOs   1

1.   A Winning Combination:
A Vision *with* a Strong Game Plan   11

2.   Passion: The Right Stuff   53

3.   The Trust Factor   71

4.   Communication: A Two-Way Street   101

5.   Teamwork: We Win Together   129

6.   Facing Adversity   163

7.   Adapting to Change   187

8.   Check Your Ego at the Door   205

Afterword   239

Winning the NFL Way

Introduction: It's Not About the X's and O's— It's About the CEOs

At the start of the 2004 NFL season, my wife Lynn and I represent six of the League's head coaches. To my knowledge, no other sports agency has ever had as many NFL head coaches as clients in a single season, that is, except for us. We also had six in 2002. One of them lost his job at the end of the season, so we had five in 2003. Three of those coaches held multiple titles of executive vice president of football operations, general manager, and head coach. Few coaches ever have this amount of power in the NFL.

We represent Jon Gruden, who led the Tampa Bay Buccaneers to a Super Bowl victory in January 2003; John Fox, who took the Carolina Panthers to the Super Bowl in 2004; and the Philadelphia Eagles' Andy Reid, NFL Head Coach of the Year in 2002. Another client is Mike Holmgren, who, along with General Manager Ron Wolf, led the Green Bay Packers to a team resurgence during the 1990s. After winning a Super Bowl for Green Bay, Holmgren signed an eight-year contract with the Seattle Seahawks in 1999. His contract was the largest ever for a NFL coach. Mike Sherman is also our client. Sherman was ultimately hired to replace Holmgren at Green Bay. He won more games during his first three years than any previous Packers coach. This includes Vince Lombardi and Mike Holmgren, both of whom have streets in Green Bay named after them.

John Fox made his head coaching debut in 2002 with the Carolina Panthers. In the previous season, the Panthers lost their last 15 games, an unenviable NFL record. Fox finished his first season with a 7-9 record, an astounding turnaround. He improved that record with an 11-5 season in 2003 and took his team to the playoffs and on to the Super Bowl against New England. On February 1, 2004, his Panthers lost to the Patriots in one of the most exciting games ever. A 41-yard field goal with four seconds remaining on the clock was the margin of victory in a 32-29 thriller.

In 2002, we also represented Marty Mornhinweg at Detroit. Unfortunately, in late January 2003, Mornhinweg was released by the Lions and has since signed on as assistant head coach with the Philadelphia Eagles under Andy Reid. And in January 2004, our client, Jim Mora, who was the defensive coordinator with the San Francisco '49ers signed a contract with the Atlanta Falcons as head coach.

Being an NFL head coach is the ultimate high-pressure job. An NFL head coach in the 21st century has to be all things to all people—players, assistant coaches, team owners, fans, and the media. Today, one year in the NFL is a lifetime and two years is an eternity. In previous decades and as recently as the 1960s, '70s, and '80s, the scrutiny surrounding an entire game was less than today's scrutiny of a single play. With the enormous advancement of technology in communication during the past several years, the proliferation of media coverage is mind-boggling. Unlike any other team sport, the head coach has seven days to dissect every possible reason why a game was lost.

Even in victory, there is pressure—people demand to know why the team didn't do better. So in addition to being brutalized for losing, the same treatment is given for not winning by a wider margin. No wonder when I talk to a winning coach on Monday morning, I often detect that his mood isn't much different than that of a losing coach.

I can't think of another line of work with such extreme highs and lows. Imagine a billion people with their eyes glued on you, watching you pace the sidelines as you direct your team in a heated Super Bowl contest. Nothing matches that "high." I know, because I was there with Jon Gruden until the early hours of the next morning, celebrating the Buccaneers' 48-21 triumph over the Raiders in Super Bowl XXXVII. And how well I know the "low." Later, during that same 24-hour period, I was there to console Marty Mornhinweg after he was let go by Detroit. It was a particularly painful experience for Marty because it happened six weeks after the end of the regular season. To add salt to the wound, Marty had been assured he would keep his job as the Lion's head coach in 2003. Considering the media attention, few firings are as brutal as what a deposed head coach endures. Imagine being booed by a hostile crowd of home fans. Think about the double humiliation of being fired and then having it announced on the six o'clock news.

There are thousands of football coaches (head coaches and assistants) at high schools and small colleges throughout the United States, and hundreds more in Division I college football, but there are only 32 NFL head coaches. They have been fired on an average of seven a year since 1989, and until recently there were only 30 teams. This small group of individuals at the top of the profession is indeed a rare breed.

As difficult as it is to get to the top of the football coaching profession, it's equally difficult to stay there. Team owners, fickle fans, and the unyielding media show little patience with poor performance. In the four-year period of 1997–2001, there were 38 instances in which a team played its first full season under a new man. During the entire 1990s, the 30 teams in the NFL had a total of 89 head coaches. The average life span was 2.5 years, which incidentally is shorter than the average NFL player's span of 3.5 years! Of the 32 head coaches who started at the beginning of the 2002 season, 50 percent had been on their jobs two years or less. The only people I know of with a shorter life expectancy than that of NFL head coaches were those hitting the beaches on D-Day.

Not surprisingly, several of today's NFL owners made huge fortunes in commerce and industry before they bought their franchise. These wealthy, successful individuals are hard-nosed, experienced businessmen. Prior to 1990, 94 percent of all ownership of professional sports teams was by individuals whose income was derived solely from the financial successes of their team. Today, only 6 percent do! As you can see, before 1990, team owners were fully devoted to the running of their franchises—they knew every aspect of the sport, backward and forward. Today's owners are not well versed in the X's and O's, but they are all CEOs! These result-driven businessmen won't tolerate failure. And when it comes to firing nonperformers, they are not bashful! A billionaire franchise owner has no qualms about discharging a multimillion-dollar-salaried head coach with several years remaining on his contract.

In spite of the short life span of the job, an NFL head coach who does his work exceedingly well is leadership personified. Done with excellence, a coach's work is poetry in motion, the choreography of a perfect ballet with each dancer executing at his or her highest level, enabling the entire troupe to achieve that magical, seemingly effortless performance. The virtuosity of a winning NFL head coach is comparable to that of a gifted conductor whose wonderful performance is the result of each musician playing at his peak to create a whole beyond the ability of any individual player. Exceptional leaders bring out the best in people in group endeavors, whether in sports, commerce, industry, or the arts.

Today's team owners recognize that no other individual contributes more to the success of the team than the head coach. In the same manner that a new CEO is hired to turn around a struggling company, a new head coach is hired to reverse the fortunes of a losing NFL team. A chief executive who is expected to produce in exchange for his fat paycheck knows the pressures put on the head coach to get results—yesterday.

When I look at the winning attributes the job requires, I believe that a head coach must be, first and foremost, a great teacher. I strongly believe that without outstanding teaching skills, one cannot succeed as an NFL head coach. Teaching skills are far more important to a coach than being a former star player in the NFL. Being an ex-NFL star player is actually a detriment, preventing him from being able to fully understand the coaching side of the game because he comes from an entirely different perspective. This is why I don't represent anyone with this background.

A winning coach must be adept at motivating people to do their best. He must excel at picking and choosing the right people—individuals who will work harmoniously with other members of the organization, making sure each person's job synchronizes with everyone else's. The head coach must be an excellent communicator. Then, too, he must be a disciplinarian, a visionary, and a person of excellent character; he is expected to serve as a role model within the organization as well as in the community at large. His job assignment is to lead a group of men with diverse backgrounds to work together in pursuit of a common goal. None of the above attributes has anything to do with X's and O's. Likewise, good leadership in business doesn't exclusively rest on one's knowledge of the nuts and bolts.

When you compare the work of a CEO with that of an NFL head coach, there are striking similarities. For example, both perform in highly competitive arenas. Like a CEO, the head coach brings together a group of diverse individuals to work in harmony in order to achieve a common goal. Both are held accountable—a head coach's performance is measured by short-term benchmarks—each Sunday's game, which is either a win or a loss. In the business arena, CEOs also have short-term benchmarks. Their performance is judged by quarterly profits, and, in some industries, by weekly results. For example, in the automobile industry, weekly reports are made comparing car sales against last year's weekly sales. Similarly, in the retail sector, the investment community on a monthly basis charts same-store sales against monthly results from the previous year.

The CEO and head coach make decisions that are not always popular; in fact, there are always hordes of fans at hand to second-guess the coach's calls. Fans aren't shy about making their disapproval known—even after the fact. Certainly, a CEO can identify with the pressure put on a head coach as he paces back and forth on the sidelines, faced with a difficult call. Ironically, the coach who must quickly make his decision in full view of a multitude of viewers, at that instant, acts alone. He's out there by himself. As business leaders often attest, it can be very lonely at the top. Much like the head coach on the sidelines, a CEO sits alone at his desk in the high-rise office building faced with difficult decisions only he can make. Like a head coach, a CEO understands that *the buck stops at his desk*. This may explain why, according to national surveys, NFL football is ranked every year as the number one spectator sport among American business leaders.

Akin to a business leader who seeks to win market share in a competitive marketplace, a determined head coach must lead his team to win over a succession of equally determined foes, week after week for 16 regular-season games. Competition intensifies in post-season games. Like a company with dominant share in its market segment, a division-leading team must fend off a hungry pack of adversaries seeking to steal its lead. Then too, a team with a poor record must strive to overtake stronger teams in the division, just as a small company seeks to take market share from a competitor that dominates the market. Good head coaches are also masters at dealing with adversity; after each defeat—no matter how devastating—they must inspire their players to pick themselves up to compete again another day.

Like corporate America, NFL team owners recognize the need for strong leadership, and they are willing to pay top dollar for it. While salary caps have been put on players, none exists for coaches. Like Fortune 500 CEOs, today's top NFL coaches are paid multimillion-dollar salaries for their leadership abilities. Several NFL franchisees believe a great head coach is well worth his upper seven-figure paycheck. In fact, some team owners believe that to land the ultimate head coach, they must not only pay millions, but trade players as well—a case in point is the Tampa Bay Buccaneers' acquisition of Jon Gruden! At the time, it seemed outrageous to trade two first- and two second-round draft choices *and* pay $8 million to Oakland for a young, 38-year-old head coach. However, when the Buccaneers' season ended with a Super Bowl victory, it was hailed as the greatest bargain since the Louisiana Purchase!

With the many parallels that exist between football and business, it is understandable that football nomenclature has invaded the workplace. You hear it everywhere—at business conferences, in committee and board meetings, in the executive dining room. Terms such as "blocking and tackling" are used to remind us to stick to the basics; "quarterbacking" is used for the function of directing people; a "goal line stand" is another way of saying a tough position must be taken when, say, negotiating an important contract; you may be forced to "punt" when another alternative is not available; and marketing people often "blitz" the public with a strong advertising campaign. The words of Lee Iacocca, spoken more than two decades ago when he pleaded with the federal government to intervene so that Chrysler could "play on a level field," have echoed throughout the corporate world ever since. Yes, the game of football is deeply ingrained in the fabric of our corporate culture.

It's a two-way street, of course. Astute NFL head coaches study the tactics of business leaders. Green Bay's Mike Sherman, for instance, finds similarities in his job as a head coach to what Jim Collins espouses in his best-selling business book, *Good to Great*. "I've never read a book that reflects my philosophy so well," says Sherman. "Especially when Collins writes about the importance of enjoying what you do and the people with whom you work. I concur—do that and the results will come."

To date, I have represented eight NFL head coaches, and in this role, I've had a front row seat allowing me to observe the best of them in action. For the past decade, I have spent thousands of hours working with my clients, one-on-one, and I count these men among my closest friends. I know them well. I know their quirks, their superstitions. Most important, I know their philosophies and work ethics. I even know what they eat for breakfast. And while I have never claimed humility as one of my strong suits, I am humbled by the brilliance in the manner that they handle the enormity of their jobs. I emphasize that while it is true they share certain common denominators, each man is quite different, with a unique style of his own.

Their leadership techniques run the gamut, and it is the differences I find interesting. Over the years, I have concluded there is no cut-and-dried formula for leadership. Having spent 25 years as a high school and junior college history teacher, I have studied the biographies of great leaders: individuals like George Washington, Abraham Lincoln, Franklin D. Roosevelt, General George S. Patton, Harry Truman, and Martin Luther King Jr. Of note is the degree to which their styles and personality traits vary. Reflect on the differences in personality, for example, between General Patton and the Reverend Martin Luther King Jr., yet each was a great leader. Similarly, Jon Gruden and Andy Reid with their contrasting personalities are both exceptional head coaches.

We tend to associate good leadership skills with charisma. Unquestionably, charisma is a factor—the attractiveness, personality, and speaking ability of former U.S. President Ronald Reagan presented a dynamic appearance reflecting what the American public wanted in our leader. Assuredly some individuals "look" more the role of a leader than do others. So by no means am I suggesting that these innate qualities be ignored. They do contribute to one's ability to lead. Certainly, some men and women seem more gifted to lead than others.

However, an individual's good looks and charm, while beneficial, are, by themselves, superficial and have little relevance in determining one's ability to lead; otherwise the world would be run by actors. Note, for example, that one of our nation's greatest leaders, Abraham Lincoln, was not considered particularly attractive. Franklin D. Roosevelt was the only U.S. president to serve for three consecutive terms—and he was handicapped—he did it in a wheelchair. For the purpose of this book, I will not elaborate on unchangeable characteristics—I am interested in substance—leadership qualities that can be emulated. Based on my observations, I surmise there is no definitive model for strong leadership. This means you can pick and choose cafeteria-style from specific qualities and traits of the five head coaches featured in this book, taking the best from each, based on what works for you. Observe how they get their people to share their vision and stick to a game plan. Learn from them how to build trust in people, and win loyalty—from employees and customers alike. Be sure to note that teamwork isn't limited to team sports; it's also applicable in the workplace. Emulate their strengths to deal with adversity as you take on your competition. And, as an NFL head coach adapts to constant change, so must every business leader in order to stay ahead of the competition. Finally, truly great leaders don't let their egos get in their way. Rather than taking credit for their successes, they are quick to give it to others.

It is my privilege and pleasure to introduce to you my clients—men who rank among the most elite in the coaching profession. Please join me and come behind the scenes to view what it is that builds a winning football team. I invite you to scrutinize their modus operandi, borrow something from this coach and something else from that coach, and in turn lead *your* team to victory.

1

A Winning Combination: A Vision *with* a Strong Game Plan

"Capital isn't scarce; vision is."

—SAM WALTON

"Setting a goal is not the main thing. It is deciding how you will go about achieving it and staying with that plan."

—TOM LANDRY

Corporate legends abound about CEOs who have a vision assuring future market dominance. I recall that one such mogul, founder of a retail apparel chain, experienced his vision on a mountaintop in Colorado. Another visionary, the wealthy owner of automobile dealerships, was sailing alone at sea amidst a ferocious storm that nearly capsized his boat, when his revelation came. While visions of this nature enhance corporate folklore, I suspect they are dramatically exaggerated. I believe it more likely that a vision begins with a vague idea that slowly evolves over time, repeatedly changing form before fully crystallizing.

When Sam Walton, founder of Wal-Mart, opened a small Ben Franklin store in Newport, Arkansas, shortly after World War II, his aim was merely to outsell his across-the-street competition. His goal was to be the town's number one five-and-ten-cent store. When he lost his lease in 1950, he moved to Bentonville where he opened Walton's Five and Dime. Walton had no plans of grandeur—the thought of becoming the world's largest retailer had not entered his mind. Walton just wanted the best five-and-dime store in Bentonville. After he opened other small stores, he gradually upgraded his vision to operating the biggest chain store in Arkansas. When one success followed another, Walton refined and elevated his purpose. Sam Walton didn't start out wanting to be the world's largest retailer, nor was it his ambition to be the world's largest company. Yet, at the end of 2003, that's exactly what Wal-Mart had become.

I have read the biographies of many Fortune 500 CEOs, and I don't recall a single one who started out with a lofty vision of someday being the top honcho. People who have low entry jobs are more focused on their current position, and only after doing well do they set their sights on advancement. They repeat this process as they advance up the corporate ladder. Having a grand vision of the future is a good thing, but it's more realistic to establish a series of smaller goals, and as you achieve one, set your sights higher on yet another. Remember too, you can alter your vision as you go along.

So, rarely does one start out with a well-defined, giant-sized vision. More often, an individual begins with an attainable vision followed by a series of still more attainable visions, and continually raises the bar with each achievement along the way. In the beginning stages, their visions are nothing more than abstract thinking. However, with a game plan, men and women implement such visions into something quite concrete. Think about it. Doesn't every success start in one's mind? More than 10 million copies have been sold since Napoleon Hill wrote *Think and Grow Rich* in 1937. In his classic book, Hill stated, "What the mind can conceive, man can achieve." He espoused that every achievement begins with an idea.

For example, when our forefathers founded our nation in 1776, they didn't have a vision of America in the 21st century. How could they? They did, however, have a conceptual vision about the freedom that future generations would enjoy. Likewise, when the Computing-Tabulating-Recording Company was founded in 1911, a firm that later changed its name to IBM, founder Thomas Watson Sr. could not have possibly envisioned that his business would evolve into today's multibillion-dollar international computer company.

Certainly having a vision provides direction. The vision by itself, however, must be followed up with a game plan. And it is the game plan that provides a road map for how to move forward to one's destination. Bear in mind that there is an important difference between a vision and a game plan. Your game plan pertains to the specifics of how to achieve your vision. Hence it is about implementation.

IN MY CASE, THERE WAS no dream in the middle of the night. No light bulb suddenly came on revealing how I could someday be a sports agent for NFL coaches. In fact, nothing in my life remotely suggested this was my calling. I played varsity football for two years at Santa Clara University, making football my number one priority. Then something happened to me in my sophomore year that replaced my thoughts of football. I took a history course taught by Professor George Giacomini, a brilliant educator who made me want to be a historian. That's right, he *made* me. He was so excited about history that I figured, "If anyone can be so enthusiastic, so committed, and so passionate about something, I've got to know more about it."

I majored in United States history, and for the next 25 years, I taught history to several thousand high school and junior college students. If I have impacted a single student the way Professor Giacomini influenced my life, I will consider myself to have had a successful teaching career.

I WILL SPARE YOU THE blow-by-blow details of my first years out of college. Let's fast-forward to my life as a married man with children when I was teaching high school at Santa Teresa High School, a public high school in San Jose, California. At this point, I was also chairman of the history department. Those were very good years for me. I taught history, which I loved, and to supplement my income I also coached football—my second passion. I loved my work. There was only one hitch. With a growing family, we had to budget our money and watch every penny. To make ends meet, I opted to receive my teaching salary over a 10-month period, and I taught history courses at junior college and high school during the summer months to supplement my income. But in 1978, the State of California elected to reduce taxes for homeowners and, as a result, massive budget cuts were made with police and fire departments, libraries, and schools coming out on the short end. While I didn't lose my full-time teaching job, my summer teaching jobs were eliminated. For a while, I sold real estate, and one year as a part-time agent, my sales commissions were $30,000, nearly equal the $35,000 I was paid for teaching and coaching.

In the mid-1970s, Santa Teresa High School and Oak Grove High

School became sister schools, sharing the same building with double sessions. As a consequence, Rich Campbell, a gifted athlete at Oak Grove, became the quarterback at Santa Teresa, where I taught and coached. A football standout, in his senior year he was one of the most sought after high school quarterbacks in the country. As his mentor, I helped him choose the University of California. Rich went on to be an All-American, and in his senior year, he asked me to be his agent. He signed with the Green Bay Packers as the sixth pick in the first round—the first quarterback to be drafted in 1981. He received a contract worth $1.25 million with a half-million-dollar signing bonus. Back then, my commission on this single transaction exceeded my annual teacher's salary. To my knowledge, no other high school teacher has ever represented anyone who was a first-round NFL draft choice.

While at Santa Clara University, I majored in American history with an emphasis diplomatic history. This education prepared me to understand negotiation, mediation, and arbitration, an ideal background for dealing with sports teams. Plus, all of my life I had played football, coached football, and counseled athletes. My experience as a real estate agent and insurance broker provided a good foundation for contractual work I do today.

Having an athlete like Rich Campbell fall into my lap was truly a blessing. Hundreds of sports agents never in their entire career represent an athlete of this caliber. A lot of people credited it to dumb luck, saying it couldn't happen again in a hundred years. But it did—two years later in 1983. Dave Stieb, who was a punter at Oak Grove, was also a star baseball player. I coached his older brother Steve at Oak Grove High School. Dave also asked me to be his agent. Dave pitched for the Toronto Blue Jays for 15 years and was a seven-time All-Star—a record for a major-league starting pitcher. During the

1980s, several other athletes approached me to be their agent. I also represented Mervyn Fernandez, a San Jose State football standout named player of the year in the Canadian League. In 1986, I met Al Davis for the first time when Fernandez jumped leagues and received a signing bonus to don an Oakland Raiders uniform. That same year, I represented Nick Vanos, a seven-foot, two-inch center for nearby Santa Clara University. Nick was drafted by the Phoenix Suns but would tragically die in a plane crash.

Later in the '80s, when I was working with a law firm that reviewed contracts for my sports agency work, one of the paralegals approached me.

"Would you be interested in representing my nephew, Don Beebe, from Chadron State?" she asked. "He's a wide receiver from the small school in Nebraska. There's a problem though. I think he may be too small for the NFL. He's only 5' 11" and weighs 175. But he's a real speedster."

"How fast is he?" I asked.

"He runs the 40 in 4.2."

"I'd like to meet him, but are you sure it wasn't 5.2 seconds?"

I knew his size hurt his chances of getting into the NFL, but I had to be in Chicago anyway, and Don agreed to meet me there with his wife, Diana.

"You're really that fast?" I asked him.

"Do you want me to prove it to you?"

"I believe you, but yes, I'd like some confirmation."

He entered, unattached, the Kansas Relays, and sure enough, he ran in near world-record time. The Buffalo Bills drafted him in the third round, and he enjoyed a 10-year career in the NFL. Beebe is one of only three players to have played in six Super Bowls.

I also represented Robin White, who won the U.S. Open doubles for women in 1988. So there I was, a history teacher moonlighting as a sports agent to make extra money. And there I was, representing world class athletes: a first-round quarterback draft choice in the NFL, an All-Star baseball pitcher, an MVP of the Canadian Football League, a starting center in the NBA, and a doubles champion in the U.S. Open. It was incredible—if you read it in a novel, it wouldn't seem believable.

THE NEXT STEP IN MY budding sports agenting career occurred, however, when I met another high school teacher who also taught history and coached football. I previously knew Mike Holmgren only by reputation. Three years my junior, he was a star quarterback at Lincoln High School in San Francisco, the "Prep Player of the Year" in 1965. A 3,592-yard passer in his senior year, he was one of the most highly recruited football players in the country. Holmgren received a full ride at the University of Southern California.

With O. J. Simpson in the backfield, the Trojans were a running team; as a result the six-foot-five Holmgren spent most of his college days warming the bench while Coach John McKay used quicker, smaller quarterbacks. He was also cursed with a dislocated thumb, sprained ankle, and a shoulder injury during his senior year. Even so, in 1970, he was an eighth-round draft choice of the then St. Louis Cardinals. His pro career as a player was short-lived, lasting only one year. He then returned to his alma mater, Lincoln High School, to teach history and coach football. In 1975, he took a teaching and coaching job at Oak Grove High School. I was teaching at Santa Teresa High School, and at the time, we were on double session with Oak Grove because my school's building was under construction.

The two schools shared the same facilities; from 7:00 A.M. to noon, our football team practiced while Oak Grove students attended classes. Then we reversed it—our students attended classes from 1:00 to 5:00 P.M. and their team practiced. During this period, Mike Holmgren and I became good friends.

In 1980, five years after his arrival at Oak Grove, he said to me over lunch, "I've been offered a job as the offensive coordinator / quarterbacks coach at San Francisco State. Everyone I've talked to so far tells me I'd be out of my mind to take it. Still I wanted your opinion, Bob. Should I take it?"

At the time, Mike and Kathy had twin daughters and she was pregnant with a third child. Taking the new job would mean taking a hefty cut in pay.

"Mike, football is your passion," I said. "Take a leave, and if it's not for you, then you can get your job back."

"Everyone else tells me not to do it. You're the only one who thinks differently. They tell me to stick with my present high school job."

"You're a brilliant coach, Mike," I assured him. "The best I've ever seen. Take the opportunity and run with it. If you pass it up, you may regret it the rest of your life."

"Thanks for the vote of confidence," he replied. "I needed that."

"While we're at it, Mike, I'd like your opinion on something," I said. "I've been thinking about becoming a sports agent. The Campbell family talked to me about representing their son. What do you think?"

"Go for it," he answered. "You're a natural. You have their trust, and in my opinion that's everything."

Holmgren took the job, and one year later moved on to coach quarterbacks at Brigham Young University. During his four-year stint at BYU, he worked under the great head coach Lavell Edwards. He also worked with Cougars quarterback Steve Young, the future All-Pro who played with the San Francisco '49ers. In 1984, Brigham Young had a 13-0 record and was the top-ranked college football team in the country.

In 1986, Holmgren signed on with the '49ers as quarterbacks coach, where he worked with Joe Montana, one of the all-time best NFL passers. He also had the good fortune to work under legendary head coach Bill Walsh, the man credited with being the innovator of the West Coast offense, a strategy that calls for a strong passing game, with many quick, short passes geared to result in long runs by receivers. In 1989, Holmgren was named the team's offensive coordinator. That same year, Holmgren's unit led the NFL in total offense. He was a hot property and other teams pursued him with head coach offers. Up until this point, I had been advising him strictly as a friend because in those days few head coaches—much less, assistant coaches—were represented by an agent.

At this point in his career, he asked me to be his agent and I agreed. I got him a richer contract with the '49ers as an offensive coordinator than many NFL head coaches received. I realized it was a good time to represent NFL coaches, because players' salaries had begun to escalate and coaches' salaries were lagging behind. They would, I figured, have to balance out eventually because, as I recognized, head coaches were undervalued. As a consequence, I decided to specialize in representing coaches rather than players.

During Holmgren's tenure with the team, the '49ers posted a 71-23-1 record, and were in postseason games for five consecutive years. San Francisco beat Cincinnati in Super Bowl XXIII and the following year beat Denver in Super Bowl XXIV.

As the '49ers' offensive coordinator, Holmgren earned such a sterling reputation that he was better known than most NFL head coaches. It was just a matter of time before he would be tapped for a head coach position. Predictably, in 1992, he left San Francisco to coach the Green Bay Packers. He did it without ever having been a head coach at the high school or college level.

It wasn't long after the new year 1992 had began when Mike Holmgren stood in the lobby of the Packers' reception area waiting to be interviewed for his first job as a head coach. A large mural, a collage of the all-time great Packers players and coaches, instantly caught his attention. His eyes focused on the team's celebrated head coach, Vince Lombardi. In the nine years that Lombardi had been in Green Bay, starting in 1959, the team amassed a phenomenal 98-30-4 record, including an unprecedented winning streak of nine playoff games. Under Lombardi, the team had won five world championship titles (1961, '62, '65, '66, and '67). No wonder the Super Bowl winner is the recipient of the Vince Lombardi Trophy, the highest honor in professional football. A quarter of a century had passed at the time of Holmgren's arrival in Green Bay, and no Packers coach had come close to filling Lombardi's shoes. The great coach died in 1970 at age 57; over the years, Lombardi has been lionized. Millions of football aficionados hail him as the game's greatest head coach ever.

"Standing there, I thought about some of the coaches that followed Lombardi," Holmgren recalls, "Dan Devine, Bart Starr, and Forrest Gregg. None had a career coaching record that exceeded .500. Lombardi's was an amazing .758. Starr and Gregg had played under Lombardi, and had been close to him. It was natural they'd try to emulate him, but he set an almost impossible standard. So when I came for my interview, I thought to myself that I was not a part of the old Green Bay Packers. In fact, I had never met Coach Lombardi.

"Even as a high school coach," Holmgren continues, "I always believed that it was more important to be who you are than to try to be someone else. This way, you're not going to con anybody. You are who you are, and if that works, fine, and if it doesn't, that's fine too. The important thing is to be true to yourself. This was my thinking going into the interview. While the standard was set, and the Packers' tradition was in place, I made a conscious decision that I couldn't be anyone else. And certainly not Coach Lombardi. Those coaches that followed him were fine men, but I think they tried to do it like Coach Lombardi did it. There's only one Coach Lombardi. In his era, there was a group of players that played for him, and it was a special thing that worked. But to try to do it exactly the same way, I believed, couldn't work."

The 1992 football season coincided with the beginning of my 25th year as a high school teacher. Brian, the youngest of our brood, was also entering his senior year. With the last of our children out of the house, my wife Lynn and I decided the timing was right for me to retire from the field of education and become a full-time sports agent. Lynn, a stay-at-home mom, had worked the past ten years helping me build my agency. With the children out of the house, she would be able to devote more time to our company. I felt I had enough experience as a sports agent that it was now time to leave teaching altogether. Considering what I had achieved as a part-time agent, I could envision a successful full-time career. Why not? I'd have an extra 40 hours a week to put into it. Giving it my undivided attention, I was confident, I would succeed.

Holmgren coached the Packers from 1992 to 1998, having a 75-37 (.670) regular season record, a 9-5 postseason mark, and two Super Bowl appearances, including a 35-21 victory over the New England Patriots in Super Bowl XXXI. His streak of winning at least one post-season game for five consecutive years (1993–97) tied him with John

Madden (1973–77) for an NFL record. When Holmgren's Packers won the Super Bowl at the end of the 1996 season, they were the NFL's leader in scoring with a team record of 456 points, as well as the League's leader in defensive scoring, a feat that had not been accomplished since 1972. The city of Green Bay was so delighted, a street was named after him—Holmgren Way. The immortal Vince Lombardi is the only other Green Bay coach to have such an honor. Appropriately, the two streets intersect.

In 1999, the Seattle Seahawks, owned by Paul Allen, America's third wealthiest individual, made an offer to Holmgren that he couldn't refuse. We negotiated a contract specifying that Holmgren would hold the position of executive vice president of football operations/general manager and Head Coach. It was an eight-year deal, the richest coach's contract in the history of football. So there we were, 20 years later, two good buddies and former high school teachers— Mike Holmgren had become one of the most respected head coaches in the NFL, and I, the owner of a thriving sports agency.

"UPON ARRIVING IN SEATTLE, I talked to the entire organization," Mike Holmgren says. "Everybody. The players, the coaches, the front office people. I had a vision of where I wanted the team to be in the future, and it was important that I share my vision with them. With an eight-year contract, I had some time to build, which is somewhat of a luxury for an NFL head coach. With a short-term contract, you're under the gun to get immediate results. You've got to produce quickly in order to keep your job, and that forces you to make short-term decisions that can come back to haunt you in the long run.

"I talked about how we were going to build our team, and what we could anticipate that would happen along the way. I explained how we were going to get through the tough times that lie ahead. 'If we stay the course,' I said, 'this should eventually work.' I had a vision of what I hoped we would be in the future, and it was important to have everyone believing we were going to do it."

With his success at Green Bay, Holmgren had established a reputation as one of the most knowledgeable head coaches in football. This gave him a lot of creditability when he became head coach at Seattle in 1999. When Holmgren talked, people listened—and most important, they believed.

" 'We're going to turn this team around like we did at Green Bay,' " Holmgren explained to his new team. "To do that, I made clear how much I needed them. 'We must depend on everyone in this room to make a contribution to our ultimate success,' I said. 'Our vision is to win the Super Bowl, and with everyone doing his best, we will do it. At Green Bay, it wasn't about me. It wasn't about Brett Favre. *It was about everybody.* We will deal with some tough things together. And we are going to share in the wonderful win at the end together. Every one of you must be a part of the team. We can only succeed by doing it together.' "

In his first season, the Seahawks finished the regular season with a 9-7 record, the team's best since 1990. The season also marked the Seahawks' first playoff game since 1988. It meant Holmgren coached games in seven consecutive postseasons, putting him behind only Tom Landry (nine years and eight years) and Chuck Noll (eight years). In 2000, his second season at Seattle, Holmgren endured his first losing season as a head coach, posting a 6-10 record. He chalked it up to a year of molding a young team that had an NFL record-high 17 rookie or first-year players. In 2003, Holmgren led the Seahawks to a 9-7 season; however, the team lost to Green Bay 33-27 in an overtime playoff game. Sometimes it is necessary to take a step backward in order to go forward to realize your vision. The Seahawks are now strong contenders for a Super Bowl title.

LIKE HOLMGREN, MIKE SHERMAN, WHO took over as head coach at Green Bay in 2000, had never been a head coach. He had spent two years with the Packers in '97 and '98 as the tight ends and assistant offensive line coach before heading west to Seattle with Holmgren. In Seattle, Sherman was an offensive coordinator and tight ends coach. In 2000, he returned to Green Bay as the team's new head coach and led the Packers to a 9-7 record. One year later, his title was changed to executive vice president/general manager/head coach. In 2001 and 2002, he had back-to-back 12-4 records during the regular seasons. Although he worked under Holmgren for three years, Sherman's philosophy about having a vision differed from that of his mentor.

"The ultimate prize in the National Football League is the Vince Lombardi Trophy given to the team that wins the Super Bowl," Sherman states. "Its namesake is a product of the Green Bay Packers, or the Packers are a product of him—whatever way you want to look at it. The local citizenry call Green Bay, 'Title Town.' This tells you how important football is to the community. The people who work in this organization—a coach, player, trainer, administrator, or maintenance person—understand what this means. Around here, it's not winning games that you're measured by—you're measured by winning championships. There is a very high expectation level. When you come into our facility, you can feel the high level of achievement that drives us. I think people will jump to the level that you make them jump to. In Green Bay, we jump very high.

"So it doesn't require any effort on my part to get anyone to buy into a vision of winning the Super Bowl," Sherman continues, "because in Green Bay, it's a built-in vision. We're expected to win. More importantly, it is imperative that I get everyone to buy into my concept of success and the principles that apply to success. I want to share the actual process of what it takes to win on a daily basis. It takes discipline, day in and day out, and that discipline has to last. At summer camp, we're doing things organizationally the way I want, but 16 games into the season, things can get a little sloppy, that is, if you don't demand the same thing every day from your people and yourself. This is what I mean by 'a concept of success,' which to me is a process. So you might say I'm more into sharing a process versus sharing a vision. And the process we share is reiterated. You cannot repeat that process to the people involved too many times. It needs to become a part of them.

"I think it's difficult for the players to think very far down the road," Sherman adds. "I want them to think in the present. One practice at a time. One play at a time. One game at a time. Don't concern yourself with what happened before or what you think will happen next. Stay in the present and deal with that because that is all that matters. At the risk of using a worn cliché, I believe you have to take it one step at a time. These step-by-step processes are the concepts I talk about to my people that I believe apply to winning."

WHEN ANDY REID BECAME HEAD coach with the Philadelphia Eagles in 1999, he inherited a team with a 3-13 record, the worst in the NFL that season. "The team was as low as you can get," he says. "The only team that picked higher than us in the draft was the Cleveland Browns and they were an expansion team.

"I had a vision of what I thought this team could be," Reid says, "and I made it crystal-clear to everyone in this organization what it was. I let them know I believed we could win football games, in spite of the previous year's poor showing. I emphasized that we had fine athletes, and with some changes that I planned to make, we could win football games. I think that's important because it provided direction. People like direction. I'm not just talking about the guy in the NFL, this is true from the guy in business to the guy who's unemployed. When people have an opportunity to see that direction and work through it, I think they're likely to succeed. Around here, everyone knows how I plan to do the things that must be done to succeed. I've brought them in to share my vision during the beginning stages, and they've taken ownership in it. It became their vision too."

Philadelphia's Brad Childress, offensive coordinator, says, "From the very beginning when Andy came here for a job interview, he sold his vision to Eagles owner Jeffrey Lurie. Andy took a thick binder to that first meeting. The binder contained hundreds, maybe even thousands, of notes he'd written down and accumulated ever since he started his coaching career. The notes he wrote weren't about the X's and O's. They covered everything from listening to suggestions by players and coaches, travel tips for team trips, marketing ideas, and so on. You name it, and Andy had it filed in his binder. At the interview, Andy laid out a plan about what he would do to make the vision he had for the team become a reality. Lurie was so impressed, he still talks about it.

"It's nice to have a vision," Childress adds, "and I agree on the value in sharing it with your people. But Andy took it to the next level because he had the plan to make his vision happen. If you have only a vision but no plan, you'll have a lot of people thinking that it's just a sales job. They'll say, 'Of course, I'd like that, but how are you going to do that?'

"When Andy first got here, he assembled a coaching staff—a group of individuals who believed in his vision. Then he recruited the kind of players he believed could fulfill his mission," Childress continues. "Sure, he wanted players with great athleticism, but he mainly sought out character guys. This is a tough business. He wanted the kind of guys that he knew would buy into his vision, and in the hard times, they would do it his way. He didn't want to be seduced by somebody's sheer athleticism who had bad character. That individual wouldn't fit in. He wanted good people, guys who are outstanding citizens—guys who are going to follow the way we do business."

AS THE SON OF A Notre Dame assistant coach, Jon Gruden says, "I grew up knowing exactly what I wanted to do. The thrill of victory, the agony of defeat were a big part of my upbringing. When I was in high school, I realized how big, how fast, how strong you had to be to play at a school like Notre Dame. Being there at the front end of the stick, I knew I would never be good enough to play for a living, but I loved football and I wanted to be a coach. My dad was my role model, and I started to apply myself in every way I could to learn from the best possible people. Early on, I never envisioned myself as a head coach. My vision was to someday be a quarterback coach. To make my vision happen, I knew I'd have to be around the smartest and the best guys. I was blessed to work under great coaches like Mike Holmgren, Walt Harris, and Johnny Majors. I learned everything I could from them. I knew that if I worked hard, I would someday get the opportunity to interview for a bigger job. Well, some opportunities eventually came my way, and I was always trying my best to take advantage of them."

Upon his arrival in Tampa, Gruden didn't talk a lot about his vision of the Buccaneers of the future. This surprised many people in the organization because it was widely believed that the one reason Gruden was brought to Tampa Bay was to win the Super Bowl. That was his assignment. Take the team to the next level. But instead of embellishing on the vision of team owners—Malcom Glazer and his three sons, Bryan, Joel, and Edward—Gruden accentuated the basics, repeatedly stating, "We win as a team. We are in this together." He was incessantly challenging every player, every coach, every person in the entire Tampa Bay organization, to "be the best you can be."

It's interesting that Gruden didn't share a vision about winning the Lombardi Trophy. Instead he presented a vision of how an organization would be built in which everyone performed at his or her highest level in a coordinated effort. He stressed that the synergy of everyone pulling together in the same direction would get maximum results. Gruden didn't have to talk about a championship season for the Buccaneers. That would be the end result of peak performances by every individual.

It was only after the team won Super Bowl XXXVII in 2003 that Gruden started talking about a grand vision of the future. This is when he started talking about making Tampa Bay a global franchise. After winning the Lombardi Trophy, Gruden has since preached to the team, "We want to become global. We want this flag, this little logo right here to be recognized by everyone, everywhere." He points to the team flag on his cap. "I want everyone in the world to know what it is. You won't even have to write 'Tampa Bay Buccaneers.' The instant they see this logo, they'll know what is. That's the vision I see for all of us. They'll instantly think about excellence. That's what the Buccaneers' logo stands for. The very best."

When Gruden gets going in front of his team, they share his

enthusiasm, and they share his vision. They are fired up when he tells them, "We are going to take it all the way. We are going to win the world championship and we're not going to look back. We are going to blaze a new trail. We are going to keep blazing. We are going to keep getting better. Guys, let me tell you something . . . it's going to get scary."

"COACHING FOOTBALL IS A COMPETITIVE profession," John Fox explains, "so I think *most* of us strive to be at the top. However, I think it's dangerous to have your sights set on a head coach's job before you're ready for it. I never had a vision of someday being a head coach when I first started out. I was content taking it one step at a time and enjoying what I was doing at the time. Besides, what I enjoyed the most about coaching were things that head coaches did only on a limited basis.

"Meanwhile, I was blessed to be around some great coaches such as Al Davis and Chuck Noll. At San Diego State, I played under Ernie Zampese who is considered an offense guru today, but back then he was a defense guru. As a graduate assistant at San Diego, I learned a lot from him. It's interesting because Zampese never wanted to be a head coach. Later in 1989, when I interviewed for my first NFL job as a secondary coach position with the Steelers, head coach Chuck Noll asked me what my coaching goals were. I answered, 'Number one, I want to be in the National Football League, and second, I have a vision to someday be a coordinator.'

" 'What about an NFL head coach?' Noll asked.

" 'No, I'd like to be a coordinator.' I answered, remembering how content Zampese was, who could have had a head coach job had he desired one.

"Then, after banging around as a defensive backfield coach, and spending seven years as a defensive coordinator, I was seeing a lot of my friends becoming head coaches. So being a head coach became a challenge to me. I looked back to all the successes and failures of individuals that I grew up with, and suddenly I had a desire to be an NFL head coach. Interestingly, I had never been a head coach, not even in high school."

Fox's coaching career started in 1978 as a graduate assistant at San Diego State, where he had played as an Aztec defensive back. He spent the next 24 years working his way up the ranks, making stops at such remote places as Boise, Idaho; Ames, Iowa; and Lawrence, Kansas, before getting an assignment with the Pittsburgh Steelers as a secondary coach in 1989. There were four more career moves before he was named defensive coordinator for the New York Giants in 1997.

With a first-things-first approach, upon his arrival in Charlotte in 2002, Fox didn't talk about a Super Bowl vision for the Panthers. "Wins and losses are hard to predict," Fox explains, "and I didn't want to talk pie-in-the-sky with the players, particularly following a 1-15 season. Instead, I spent time talking about how we could improve— the methods that we'd incorporate to make us better."

Fox focused on a more realistic vision in which the Panthers would make many improvements during the 2002 season and build for the future. After a dispiriting season, Fox knew that his first task was to instill self-respect in his players. The Panthers were a young team. With patience, they would have their day in the sun.

"I told my coaching staff," concludes Fox, " 'I am the head coach, and in this position, I've got to create an environment for you to be better coaches and for us to have better players.' " Fox made it very clear to them—he simply told them what a good leader does.

★　★　★

SOME GAMES YOU NEVER FORGET. One that comes to my mind is the Eagles/Cowboys game on Sunday, October 3, 1999, at the old Veterans Stadium. It was the fifth game of Andy Reid's first season as head coach and he was winless. Down 10-0 when the half ended, Philadelphia looked as if they were about to lose five in a row. The Eagles had not made a first down in the entire first half.

"This is our game," Reid told the team during halftime. "They can't beat us. The Cowboys played their best football, and they're only up by 10."

Philadelphia, the City of Brotherly Love, is reputed to have the toughest fans in professional sports. They can be so mean-spirited, they'd boo Santa Claus. The crowd gets so out of control that police constantly make arrests. To save the city the time and cost of running paddy wagons back and forth to the slammer in downtown Philly, "Eagles Court" had been set up within the bowels of the stadium. With this unique court, unruly fans can be arrested, tried, and convicted, all conveniently on the premises! Nowhere else in the world does a courtroom exist inside a sports arena. In this hostile environment, Andy Reid began his first job as an NFL head coach.

As a side note, Lincoln Financial Field, the new home for the Eagles, opened at the beginning of the 2003 season. Acoustically, the stadium was designed to retain loud noise. Its winglike roof structures were constructed to actually amplify the sound of the crowd. Why increase rather than reduce noise? The louder the crowd, the more home field advantage. Its objective is to intimidate visiting teams. But wait a minute! During a losing season, can't this advan-

tage backfire? Yes, indeed! Philadelphia fans also boo their own players and coaches!

So here was where Andy Reid inherited a team with a 3-13
record. Hard-nosed Eagle fans were not about to tolerate another
losing season. There was no prior indication that Reid was the man
to turn the team around. Fans opposed team owner Jeffrey Lurie's
hiring of Reid because they wanted a high-profile, experienced head
coach with a winning record. Furthermore, one of the first things
Reid did as head coach was to select Syracuse's quarterback Donovan McNabb as the Eagles' second pick in the first round of the
1999 draft. Nobody doubted McNabb was a potential starting NFL
quarterback—they just didn't think he should have gone so high in
the draft. The general consensus in Philadelphia was that the Eagles
should have picked Ricky Williams, college football's current Heisman Trophy winner.

But what drove fans raving mad on this particular Sunday afternoon was that Reid had McNabb sitting on the bench when starting
quarterback Doug Peterson was playing atrociously. Peterson had
been a backup quarterback at Green Bay when Reid was the Packers'
quarterback coach for two years prior to coming to Philadelphia.
Reid was a big proponent of the West Coast offense, which Peterson
knew—and McNabb did not. So Reid took Peterson with him to help
break in McNabb. Peterson came to town knowing it would only be
a matter of time before McNabb would be the starting quarterback.
He was the future "franchise" player. That was the understanding
among Reid, Peterson, and McNabb. Fans fuming in the stadium,
however, were not privy to this arrangement.

Doug Peterson was an average NFL quarterback, and when
an average quarterback is having a bad day, it gets ugly in Veterans
Stadium. No first downs for an entire first half is real ugly! I must

confess I shared the same thoughts as everyone else in the packed stadium. I was also thinking, "Why does Reid have his multimillion-dollar quarterback Donovan McNabb sitting on the bench?" The fans were chanting, "McNabb! McNabb!" They were vicious, shouting, "F——Reid," and other obscenities.

When 68,000 people boo and scream like raving maniacs, you can believe a head coach is having a bad day. Call that a horrendous day when you're a rookie head coach in Philadelphia. "Why isn't Reid playing McNabb?" I kept thinking. I'm Reid's agent and I felt like booing him too. He has to play McNabb. I say to myself, "Andy must know his job is on the line. The people of Philadelphia will demand his head on a plate." I'm sitting there, and I'm doing my best to restrain myself from joining the shout, "Play McNabb! Play McNabb!"

By the time I was convinced that no coach in the NFL would have kept McNabb out of the game, the whistle blew to start the second half. I was wrong. Andy Reid refused to put him in the game. As the game progressed, to the amazement of the hostile crowd, the Philadelphia defense came alive, forcing three turnovers with two interceptions and a fumble. They applied pressure on All-Pro quarterback Troy Aikman and they held in check the Cowboys' all-time greatest running back, Emmitt Smith. The Eagles turned the game around and won 13-10. This was the day that Andy Reid won the respect of Philadelphia fans. With John Madden and Pat Summeral announcing the game on national television and seeing the Eagles come from behind to beat the Cowboys, Reid also won the admiration of football fans across America.

After the Dallas game, Reid informed the media why he hadn't played McNabb. He explained that his long-term plan was to wait until McNabb was ready to be the starting quarterback and that's when he'd start him. In Reid's opinion, the Eagles' offensive line wasn't settled. He determined that playing McNabb too soon would possibly dampen the young quarterback's confidence and risk a potential injury. Reid also made it clear that his objective was to have a championship team in Philadelphia and that he would stick to his plan.

Why didn't he play McNabb? Reid was a man with a plan—and he stuck to his plan. It didn't matter what anyone else thought. He was the head coach and it was his call. He adhered to the advice inscribed on a plaque that sits on his desk. It reads: "The important thing is to lay a plan, and then follow it step by step no matter how small or large each one by itself may seem." The quote was from Charles A. Lindbergh, a man who had also followed a plan.

Then the same mean-spirited crowd who'd booed and jeered Reid earlier in the game did a complete flip-flop. In the final minutes of the final quarter, they were on their feet chanting, "Eagles! Eagles!" Andy Reid won their respect that day and has had it ever since. The Eagles finished with a 5-11 record in his first season, a marked improvement over the previous season.

In 2000, Reid lead the team to an 11-5 season, earning a trip to the NFC Divisional Playoffs, and again in 2001, went 11-5 and improved the Eagles' postseason play by winning two playoff games. In 2002, the Eagles tied a franchise record for most wins in a season (12). Most amazingly, Eagles Pro Bowl quarterback Donovan McNabb, as well as his backup Koy Detmer, was on the disability list for the final five games of the regular 2002 season. Using third-stringer A. J. Feeley, the Eagles were 4-1 and captured home field advantage in the NFC playoffs. With four years of NFL head coaching under his belt, Reid had the highest winning percentage (.606) in team history. Most noteworthy, he captured back-to-back division titles—a first for the franchise—and has the most postseason wins (4) of any coach in the franchise's history.

"You're going to go through some rough times," Reid explains. "If all of a sudden you flip the switch to the other direction and change offenses or defenses or philosophies midway through, you're in trouble. You lose your people. You've got to stick to your plan."

Brad Childress, the Eagles' offensive coordinator, says, "When Reid came here, he met with owner Jeffrey Lurie and president Joe Banner, and he informed them he planned to bring Doug Peterson in. 'We're going to acquire this guy,' he said, 'and he's going to teach McNabb some things he has to know. There will be a point when Donovan is ready. But not right away.' Management bought into Andy's plan."

AS MENTIONED EARLIER, MIKE HOLMGREN'S first job as head coach was with Green Bay in 1992. He had never been head coach in either college or high school! Neither had Fox, Gruden, Reid, or Sherman, who can all thank Holmgren for dispelling the idea that head coaching experience is an absolute résumé requirement for a head coach job in the NFL—the highest level in the football coaching profession. I presently represent 12 NFL coordinators and one college head coach, and it's only a matter of time before some of them will be NFL head coaches. With only 32 such positions available, grabbing hold of this elusive brass ring is an uncommon and coveted accomplishment. As their agent, I render an important service by preparing them for their job interviews.

Over a period of time, I developed a job interview process designed to show my clients at their best specifically when applying for an NFL head coach position. Remember now, since there are only a handful or so of these job openings each year, the process is infrequently used. Having said this, I modestly add that our placement ratio for clients has been quite high. Because it is proprietary information for the exclusive use of my clients, I can't go into specific details. But what I will reveal is that the process is designed to prepare my client to present himself most favorably during the entire interviewing process. It covers the smallest of details, from proper attire to what to bring to the interview. Most significant, I coach my clients on questions they should ask, as well as how to respond to questions asked. For example, they must be thoroughly abreast of everything that has been going on in the franchise, down to minute details about players, coaches, franchise history, and team performance during the most recent season.

Stories abound of candidates who bombed in an interview because they came prepared to talk only about the X's and O's, when it's already a given that they excel in this area. Besides, job interviews at this level involve meetings with team owners, who don't have a lot of interest, or, for that matter, expertise, about the X's and O's. More meaningful to franchise owners are the prospective head coach's vision and game plan. They're not interested in just a single season but instead seek insight into what to expect in the future. So while football expertise is a requisite, strong leadership skills are paramount. Our job is to make sure we put a pretty dress on a pretty girl.

A common denominator of all head coaches I represent is their preparedness and attention to detail. In short, each of them is meticulously organized. This patented quality accurately describes all five men. Having said this, I'll also state that no one has ever epitomized a man who came totally prepared to present his plan to his interviewers more than Andy Reid. In fact, the degree to which he did it has become so legendary throughout the Philadelphia Eagles organization, it is now referred to as "the Plan."

Andy Reid didn't rush to put together the Plan only after Eagles owner Jeffrey Lurie and president Joe Banner expressed interest in hiring him. Reid had begun to assemble the Plan back in 1982 as a graduate assistant at Brigham Young University when he worked under Lavell Edwards. He fastidiously took notes on everything he admired about Edwards—his wonderful human qualities that included treating everyone with respect, regardless of stature, his disciplinary skills, and his ability to keep his cool under pressure. While assembling his notes at San Francisco State University, Reid observed that head coach Vic Rowan would call a high school or college coach to inquire about an interesting play he saw during a televised game. ("To this day, I'll call an NFL, college, or high school coach about unusual plays I see on TV," tells Reid.) What he learned about unusual plays also found its way into his journal.

In 1992, by the time Reid came to the Packers to work under Mike Holmgren, he had amassed an extensive collection of thoughts and ideas he intended for use when he would be an NFL head coach. Starting first as the Packers' tight ends and assistant offensive line coach, Reid was later named quarterback coach. Under head coach Mike Holmgren, Reid's note-taking became even more intense. Longtime staff people recall Reid always asking questions and writing notes to himself. "I remember him as quiet, but with a good sense of humor," one staff member tells. "I'd describe him as a quiet observer. He wanted to know about everything so he could understand the big picture."

There was so much to learn from a man like Holmgren, whom Reid considered among the best in the profession. With back-to-back visits to the Super Bowl in 1997 and 1998, Reid knew that the time was near when he would have the opportunity to lead a team of his own. His tenure at Green Bay was highlighted when he was given the assignment to coach Brett Favre, football's premier quarterback. Reid, a former BYU player who played tackle and guard, had come a long way since his days on the line. Incidentally, Reid had been a two-way lineman in high school and, in addition, the team's punter and kicker, so he had personally experienced some offense play during his playing days. All in all, Andy Reid had a lot of exposure to the game of football. And he had tens of thousands of jotted-down notes to prove it.

His volumes of note-taking included what he liked and didn't like about all that he'd witnessed during his 16-year apprenticeship at various college and pro levels. He had accumulated information that went far beyond the X's and O's of the game. Sure, Reid had compiled hundreds and hundreds of plays, but it went much further. His notes covered the subjects of leadership; training; conditioning; travel arrangements via air, bus, and limousine; lodging; food services; public relations; slant plays; pep talks; lectures; administrative duties—name it and it appeared in Reid's head coach notebook. His notes were meticulously organized in three-ring binders. Everything was prepared and at his fingertips, ready for the day he became an NFL head coach.

When Reid sat down to discuss the job opening for a head coach's position with Philadelphia, he brought with him the Plan, a blueprint that would serve as the foundation of the Eagles' resurgence. Team owner Lurie was deeply impressed with Reid's game plan and long-term vision. Lurie described him as "a CEO on the field who understands the big picture and the short-term picture. You have to always balance the two. Disciplined. Prepared. Smart. It's an awfully good combination."

Reid got the job and he stuck to his Plan. It called for the team to have a franchise quarterback. "Doug Peterson was an important part of the puzzle," says Brad Childress, offensive coordinator for the Eagles. "Although Doug didn't have much success as an NFL quarterback, Andy brought him in because he did know the system. Of course, Andy had to sell Lurie and Banner on the importance of bringing Peterson in. It wasn't an easy sale. First, he had to convince them to go with McNabb as the team's first draft choice and, after that, to keep him on the bench until he was comfortable with the West Coast Offense. Andy stuck to his Plan. He refused to throw McNabb to the wolves."

All the pressure put on Reid didn't sway him from sticking to his conviction. Losing his first four games would have convinced a lesser coach to alter his game plan. Reid, however, never gave in to pressure. He kept his cool and stayed the course. McNabb would play only when Reid determined he was ready. It took ten games before Reid finally gave the green light to McNabb to go in as quarterback.

With several seasons under Reid's belt as head coach, the Eagles' turnaround has been one of the most remarkable in NFL history. Since his arrival, Philadelphia has become one of football's most dominating teams and most respected franchises. Still, Reid continues to work on the Plan, habitually tweaking it, always working to improve it. He continues to track thoughts and ideas in journals and notebooks. He keeps a daily schedule on an index card that's always in his hand. Still more index cards are scattered on his desk. Eventually, his secretary files each of them so he can draw on them at an opportune time. To Andy Reid, the Plan is a work in progress.

Come game time and there stands Andy Reid on the sidelines, always with his sideline sheets in hand. From these 11-by-17-inch sheets, he calls each play. They contain no diagrams—each play is a typewritten narrative. "The plays are on cardstock," tells Carol Wilson, Reid's administrative assistant, "and last season we switched to a cardstock made by another company. I couldn't believe he would notice the difference, but he said, 'Hey, this isn't the same. I need it to be exactly like it was.'

" 'I think it is, Coach. It's just a different company.'

" 'I'm telling you this is different. Please check it out, Carol.'

"Sure enough, the new cardstock was a couple of milliliters off, so I placed an order with the previous company."

MIKE HOLMGREN IS ONE OF the most organized men I have ever met. This is evident by the way he prepares his game plan prior to training camp. A man who believes that football games are won by the amount of preparation exerted prior to game time, Holmgren leaves no stone unturned during those long, hot summer weeks when the Seahawks get ready for the upcoming season. The Seahawks migrate to Cheney, a tiny town just south of Spokane where they take over the athletic facilities at Eastern Washington University.

"At summer camp," explains Holmgren, "we're in what I call our 'robot mode.' Every minute is accounted for during the entire six weeks we're in Cheney. I'm talking about every practice, every meeting, every workout in the weight room, everything. This gives everyone the freedom to do his job without any distractions. It's a very disciplined environment. And believe me, while you hear the comments that professional athletes lack discipline, they really do want it. Sure, they may grouse about it now and then. There's nothing wrong with having them complain. But they truly welcome the discipline. They know what to expect when they're at our training camp. They want to know when we are going to do this, when we are going to do that, when meals will be served, and so on."

When I first visited the Seahawks training camp in Cheney, it reminded me of a television special where producers and directors have every second accounted for in a prepared script. I compare Holmgren's training camp to putting on a six-week television special. It takes a tremendous amount of thought and effort to organize a marathon event that involves so many people. The manner in which Holmgren organizes training camp sets the stage for the entire 16-week season. Summer camp is only the beginning. Once the season is under way, Holmgren increases the pace and intensifies the game plan.

Susan Broberg was Mike Holmgren's administrative assistant during his years in Green Bay. Following Holmgren's departure to Seattle, Ray Rhodes served as the Packers' head coach for the 1999 season that ended with eight wins and eight losses. When Mike Sherman replaced Rhodes in 2000, he inherited Broberg as his administrative assistant—or, depending on your point of view, she inherited him. "Getting a new boss is a difficult transition," Broberg explains, "so I was somewhat apprehensive when Coach Rhodes was fired and I heard Coach Sherman was coming in to be interviewed. I'm sure everyone here was a little uptight. You don't know what your future will be because you're thinking, 'What if he doesn't like me? What if our personalities clash?' Even though Coach Sherman had previously been here as a tight ends coach, I hardly knew him in those days. Coach is so unassuming and humble that back then, he just went about doing his job and stayed in the background.

"Out of the clear blue sky, Coach Sherman called me before coming in for his interview," Broberg says. "He said he'd like to ask me some questions. It turned out he had many, many questions, mainly focused on what I thought about how the Packers could do things better. 'What's your read on so-and-so?' he asked. 'And how about so-

and-so?' He asked questions about the structure of the coaching staff. How were the players treated in the training room? What about in the equipment room? How did I think it could be better? What was my interpretation on this? On that? We talked for 90 minutes, and at the end of our conversation he graciously thanked me.

"When I hung up the phone, I called my husband because we had talked about some of the big-name coaches under consideration for the job, and Coach Sherman was relatively unknown. 'He's going to get that job,' I said. 'I know he's going to get that job. And I hope he's my new boss. I hope he wants to keep me.' I was so impressed with how prepared he was, and I couldn't get over that he took his time to call somebody like me in the organization to ask my advice. That was my first encounter with him. Well, he did get the job, and ever since that first conversation, he's made me feel so useful to him. And trusted—I feel so trusted by him."

Broberg says that in addition to working closely with Holmgren, Rhodes, and Sherman, she also got to know Gruden and Reid during their days as assistant coaches at Green Bay. Broberg concurs that they are all highly organized individuals, a trait she attributes to their dedication to their careers. In her opinion, Sherman is the most focused on his game plan. "He leaves no stone unturned," she states. "It starts with the way the team practices, and the same intensity permeates the organization. Coach Sherman is so detail-driven, even every road trip is planned in advance for the entire season, in fact, to such a degree that to an outsider, it would seem nonsensical. For instance, when the team travels, the coach has a seating chart prepared that determines who sits next to whom on an airplane. Why does he do this? He might want one of the doctors nearby so he can talk to him."

Sherman explains that a good game plan is all about discipline.

"We have everything planned for the entire season," he states, "and we've got to stick to our agenda on a day-by-day basis. With a 16-game season, things can get a little sloppy if you don't demand the same thing from your players and yourself. Before we play our first exhibition game, I lay out the practice schedule for the entire season. Every trip is planned in detail in advance and coordinated with our game schedule. For instance, in our 2003 season we had three Monday night games and a Sunday night game. We played Thanksgiving Day, and at the end of the season, we had two back-to-back trips on the West Coast.

Every day is planned in advance, and this allows us to stay focused, making sure nothing distracts us. There are so many things that can throw a team off track. More significant than the game on Sunday is what happens during the week preceding the game. The media can sometimes be a bigger opponent than the Minnesota Vikings or the Chicago Bears. Newspeople say many negative things and even cause divisiveness in the locker room. For instance, they might say things about a player that causes problems with his teammates. They can tackle you before you hit the field."

"WHEN I FIRST ARRIVED IN Charlotte in 2002, this thing was in bad shape," tells John Fox. "At the time, there were 31 NFL teams, and the Panthers ranked last on both sides of the ball with the worst offense and worst defense in the League. Financially, the team had maxed out on the salary caps, so we were a 1-15 team that was paying salaries like a team with a 15-1 record. The team was hurting so bad, the players' wives were embarrassed to go to the shopping malls. The players were so ashamed, they didn't want to be seen in public. You have to remember now that when you do badly in this business, the whole world knows it.

"Having lost 15 games straight, everyone in the organization was acting like they just found out they've got three months to live. Immediately upon coming here, my game plan was to build a positive environment. So I put the emphasis on the positive and looked at all the good things we had going for us. " 'We have excellent facilities,' I stressed to the organization. 'And this is a great city for recruiting purposes. Our owner-founder, Jerry Richardson, is a former All-American player and was a member of the 1959 world championship Baltimore Colts team, so we have great ownership. Now it's true there's been some poor decisions made, but there is absolutely no reason why we shouldn't win here.'

"The first thing I tried to create was a winning attitude from the top down," Fox continues. "I began with getting the owner fired up, the general manager fired up and then the team fired up. I talked a lot about how, with the right plan, hard work, and good decision-making, there was no reason why we couldn't win here.

"My plan was to win with smart, tough, better-conditioned people than the people we compete against. I announced exactly what I was looking for to win, and I set high expectations. I'm a big believer that people live up or they live down to your expectations of them. In a leadership position, you get what you expect out of people. If you don't expect much, you don't get much. However, if you expect a lot and you're consistent about expecting it, you will get a lot. The trouble is that people give themselves limitations and they build up walls that limit them. To turn the program around, I had to eliminate the losing mentality. Now and then, I brought in new personnel; for example, I changed trainers. Why? Because I wanted to be surrounded with people who shared my enthusiasm, and trainers spend a lot of time with players. I brought in several high-energy people I had worked with or knew in the past, and, most importantly, they were people with the same passion for the game that I have."

Fox made extensive changes in the Panthers coaching staff during his first few months with the team. Prior to the opening of the 2002 season, for example, he brought in Dan Henning, offensive coordinator/quarterbacks; Mike Trgovac, defensive coordinator; Rod Perry, secondary coach; Jim Skipper, running backs coach; and Sal Sunseri, defensive line coach. He continued making changes in 2003, bringing in Danny Crossman, special teams assistant and assistant strength and conditioning coach; Ken Flajole, defensive assistant; Dave Magazu, tight ends coach; and Mike Maser, offensive line coach. "I recruited people with expertise and enthusiasm," he states. "I wanted people who would share my passion and excitement so it would spread throughout the organization."

Although he had never been a head coach, Fox had an impressive record, having served as New York Giants defensive coordinator for five years prior to joining the Panthers. During that period, he built one of the greatest defensive teams in the NFL and had been honored by *Pro Football Weekly* as the 2001 Assistant Coach of the Year. His excellent track record gave him instant credibility, which, in turn, helped him sell his game plan.

At the onset of Fox's turnaround program for the Panthers, he made the bold decision to select Julius Peppers, a defensive end, as the second player to be drafted in the 2002 draft. The Panthers had made a lot of foolish mistakes that got them to the basement of the NFL. And to many, when a team with second draft choice rights takes a lineman, it's a move that adds to an already dumb and dumber reputation.

So why did Fox take Peppers?

"There was some speculation that the decision was based on Peppers coming from up the road in Chapel Hill. Believe me, taking a North Carolina player had nothing to do with anything. It was just a coincidence. We had a choice of picking a lot of people, and my philosophy on taking a quarterback is different from other coaches. Personally, I feel that you have to pay this guy like a future Hall of Famer because that's what it's going to cost. And he's yet to have played a single down in this League. Believe me, I did a lot of research before taking Peppers, more so than I've ever done in my career. With my defensive background, I could have succumbed and taken a quarterback. That would have appeased everyone as the right way to go. Had I done that, there would have been no criticism. However, when a defense guy takes a defensive lineman as his pick, it's not a popular thing to do. And had Peppers been a bust, there would have been all hell for me to pay."

As it turned out, Julius Peppers was named NFL Defensive Rookie of the Year in 2002 by the Associated Press, so a year later Fox was hailed as a genius. Incidentally, in 2003, he took Jordan Gross, an offensive tackle from Utah, as the eighth pick in the first round. "Peppers and Gross are not sexy picks," Fox says, "but I know this—you can't play offense without blocking. And you can't play defense without tackling. This is not rocket science. You can't throw the ball if you can't block. You can't run the ball if you can't block. So to me, that's where you go. Remember now, we are a work in progress. We have not arrived by any stretch."

Fox believes the only way a game plan can be executed is through preparation. "I liken it to school," he explains. "When you didn't go to class, take notes, or read your material, you knew when you went to take your test that you'd do terribly. You just knew it because you weren't prepared. You have no confidence. Now in college, you can look over the person's paper next to you and copy off it. Well, you can't do that in the National Football League. The whole world sees you. Your wife and kids see you. That big eye in the sky tells it like it is. So I'm constantly selling the team on preparation. It's all part of the game plan."

One of Fox's constant reminders to his players is: "It's a production world. Those who produce will succeed. And those who don't will fall on their face." Again, it goes back to preparation. He claims a lot of little things add up to make people prepared or unprepared. "Like taping yourself," he explains, "making sure you go to practice with nothing else on your mind, watching the films, and so on. You have to focus on what you have to do. It's not easy to stay focused in football because there are so many things going on around you to distract you. To be productive, you must be prepared. Football games aren't won on Sunday afternoons. You win them by what you do during the week."

Carolina's defensive line coach Sal Sunseri says, "Fox keeps repeating, 'If you prepare, if you are mentally tough, and you are ready, you will produce.' When it comes to feeling the heat, Coach says, 'You will either feel it, or you will apply it.'

"It's like the other day, I heard Foxy say to a player, 'The bottom line is,' he said, 'that when I'm on the practice range, man, I hit that golf ball beautifully. When I step up to the tee, I don't drive the ball the same way. Well, we've got to get to where we do it the same out on the field as we do during practice. Where it doesn't matter if we're on the practice range or the real tee. We hit that ball the same over and over again. Only through preparation does that happen.'"

★   ★   ★

JON GRUDEN CONCURS. "FOOTBALL ISN'T just games," he says. "It's about planning. We don't just twiddle our thumbs at meetings all week, we're constantly reviewing facts and putting together Sunday's game plan. I'm here at the office at four in the morning, and I'll put together a 12- to 14-page tip sheet for our quarterbacks. It presents seven or eight critical points—information about opposing players and the defenses they play. It's well documented and precise. I'll seek input from our players, more so than most other coaches. If they don't like something, I'll take it out of our game plan. If they don't buy into it, no matter how good I think it is, it isn't going to work.

"It's a long season, probably too long," Gruden continues. "A lot of these guys don't want to be here practicing on Wednesday, Thursday, and Friday, for 16, 18, 24 weeks. Some of them would rather sit in that cool chair, that cushy chair in the air-conditioning. They'd like to sit there telling stories, watching game film, and not come out here in this heat. I've got to motivate them. I've got to push them and tell them how important it is. I've got to make sure they know it's a great winning edge to know you're prepared to win. Let them know that they're going to sleep good the night before the game knowing that the plan is in place and we can execute it. Let them know, 'You have to continue to pound the rock and develop mental toughness.'"

BUSINESSPEOPLE REFER TO THEIR COMPANY strategies so frequently as their game plan that we tend to forget that the term "game plan" is sports lingo.

Unlike a vision that I distinguish as abstract thinking, a game plan is an explicit strategy that can be either short-term or long-term. Obviously, a game plan in the NFL on any given Sunday falls into the short-term category.

In the Eagles-Cowboys game played on October 3, 1999, Andy Reid's refusal to deviate from his game plan exemplifies strong leadership. Although Reid had lost his first four games as a head coach and was being unmercifully booed by a hostile Philadelphia crowd, he stuck by his game plan, refusing to cave in to the demands of the fans. As Reid pointed out, people are apt to lose confidence in a leader who changes horses midstream.

Certainly, it takes strong conviction and courage for a visionary CEO to stick to his marketing strategy while losing market share during the early stages of his game plan. Likewise, a business leader may be censured for discharging large numbers of people, closing plants, and reducing inventories in order to stop the organization's flow of red ink. There are many similarly turbulent and troubled times in the life of a business, such as the one Reid endured, that cause lesser managers to stray from their game plan. These are times when strong leaders must show their mettle and inspire their people to push on. Conversely, weak leaders act indecisively, thereby creating an atmosphere of doubt and confusion.

When Reid and Fox first presented their game plans, neither was well received. Reid's decision to pick Donovan McNabb as his first draft choice, as part of a plan to build the Eagles' offensive unit around him was disparaged by Philadelphia fans. Similarly, Fox's choice of Julius Peppers, a defensive end, as his number one draft choice was unpopular with Panthers fans. Business leaders must remember that radical change that introduces a new game plan is likely to be met with resistance. Simply put, you can expect people to resist change.

To reverse people's resistance to change, it's important to invite them to share your vision and then participate during the early planning stages of your game plan. This gives them a sense of ownership. Your vision becomes their vision. People will support a game plan that they helped to create. On the other hand, when a game plan is thrust upon people whose input was not solicited, it's probable that you will run into resistance.

I am fascinated by the degree of preparation exhibited by all of the head coaches I represent. Each is so thorough in his preparation, paying close attention to detail, leaving no stone unturned. This, too, generates confidence and inspires others to follow. Meticulous, painstaking preparation is a sign of purposefulness. In business, successful leaders are always well prepared at committee and board meetings. We've all attended meetings at which some members— even the committee chairperson—came unprepared. They talk about their grand visions—but without a detailed game plan to back it up, it's just talk.

A detailed, well-conceived game plan augments the probability that it will be supported by others. People are impressed you did your homework and consequently feel secure with your recommendations. In contrast, a haphazard, inadequately organized game plan is doomed to have poor reception, even though it may be conceptually correct. It fails to win people's confidence.

Here too, top leaders rely on strong communication skills to sell their visions. A first-rate presentation of their game plan stimulates people to buy into it. Over the years, I've seen good game plans bomb due to weak presentations. You have to sell it. After they have spent so much time preparing a game plan, I'm perplexed why people fail to allocate adequate time practicing their presenting of it. A poor presentation discourages people from supporting an otherwise excellent game plan.

Attention to details is a sign of a well-prepared game plan. A word of caution: Know your audience. Don't get so wrapped up in the X's and O's that you lose sight of the big picture. This is why I advise my clients to think long term when they present their vision during a job interview. I tell them to back it up with a detailed presentation on how their game plan will turn their vision into reality. Another word of caution: Don't overwhelm people with excessive detail that makes their heads swim. Remember, sometimes less is more.

2

Passion: The Right Stuff

"We could hardly wait to get up in the morning."

—WILBUR WRIGHT

Upon arriving at the Green Bay airport, I went directly to the baggage claim area and spotted a boyish-looking, blond-haired kid holding an 8-by-10-inch card with my name on it.

I introduced myself: "I'm Bob LaMonte. Thanks for picking me up."

"It's a pleasure to know you, Mr. LaMonte. I'm Jon Gruden," the polite young man answered. "Here, let me take your luggage."

Trim and suntanned, he looked more like a surfer or a beach boy than the typical ex-jock NFL team employee. At 225 pounds, I volunteered to carry my own luggage, but he insisted he would. What the hell, my suitcase had wheels on it, so I let him pull it.

"You're a great agent," he said enthusiastically. Then he proceeded to talk about my clients and some of the deals I negotiated for them. I was impressed with how well he had done his homework. "You go way back with Coach Holmgren I'm told," Gruden said. "You both taught high school history. My mother is a schoolteacher."

We talked nonstop until we arrived at the Packers' summer training camp a few miles down the road. At dinner that night, I mentioned to Holmgren, "Nice kid, that driver who picked me up today. We must be getting old, Mike. I thought he was a college student doing a summer internship. Quite a talker. He kept drilling me with questions."

"That's Uncle Buck."

"Uncle Buck?"

"Yeah, that's what Jerry Rice nicknamed him and it stuck. From the movie *Uncle Buck* with John Candy."

"He doesn't look anything like Candy. Candy must weigh 300 pounds."

"The Candy character slept in an old, beat-up Buick in the movie," Holmgren said. "They call Gruden Uncle Buck because when he first came to the '49ers, he slept in an old Buick Delta he picked up for $500."

"No kidding?" I said, intrigued.

"Man, he's the first one here in the morning and the last to leave. The kid's got a passion for this game like I've never seen. He has an insatiable appetite to learn everything he can about football. Extremely bright too. Mark my words, someday he's going to be a head coach."

"Really?"

"I'll tell you how I first hired him," Holmgren continued. "When I was with the '49ers, I was looking for a quality control coach, a job I figured might last six months. He was the best of the lot, but when it came time to make him a job offer I told him, 'I can't hire you because I'm asking you to make too much of a sacrifice. I don't want to do that. It's a short-term job and it doesn't pay much.'"

"'That's okay,' he said. 'I really want the job. Working for a team like the '49ers is a dream come true. I've got my heart set on it.'

"'We want to start using computers for developing our game plans so we can score them,' I explained to him. 'This has never been done in the League before. We need somebody who knows football *and* computers.'

"'I know football,' he answered. 'Been around it all my life. I was a quarterback in high school and a backup quarterback at the University of Dayton, a Division III school in Ohio. I come from a football family. Growing up, my dad was an assistant coach at Notre Dame under Dan Devine.'

"'What do you know about computers?' I asked.

"'Truthfully?' he said. 'Very little. But I can learn.'

"'I'm going on a vacation for a month. You have 30 days to learn because when I get back, you've got to know computers.' I don't know how he did it, Bob, but in that one month, he became quite knowledgeable, and before long, he was a whiz kid on the computer. He has such a strong work ethic, and you combine it with his passion for football, and I'm telling you, he'll do whatever it takes to get the job done. Another thing. He's a sponge. The guy absorbs everything he sees and hears. I have to kick him out of the office at night and make him leave. And he can't wait to get back here the next day. He's the first one here every morning."

WHEN I BEGAN MY TEACHING career, I couldn't wait to get up in the morning to conduct my classes. For the first time in my life, I was able to stand in front of an audience, and without a single note, I could talk nonstop for an entire hour.

I had been teaching classes in the evenings at San Jose City College, and one night, Dr. Murgia, the school's president was walking by my classroom and heard me lecturing on American history. He came in and sat at one of the desks with the students. He stayed for the entire hour. I was surprised he would take so much time because he was a very busy man. As students were heading out the door, he walked over to me and said, "Thank you. I've been an educator going on three decades, and that was the most interesting class I ever attended. Keep up the good work, LaMonte!"

I know my enthusiasm came through when I taught history. A teacher can tell when students are turned on. It's interesting that the word *enthusiasm* comes from a Greek word meaning "God within." I believe a person's enthusiasm is something that has to be sincere. You can't fake it because people can sense if it's real or not. When you love what you do, your enthusiasm will spread to others. As the British novelist Edward Bulwer-Lytton wrote, "Nothing is so contagious as enthusiasm."

As I mentioned, for years after I started up my agency, I continued to teach high school history. "As a teacher, you make only a fraction of what you do as an agent," a friend once said to me. "Why are you still teaching school when you can be putting that time into your agency? Think how much more money you'd make." I was never driven by money. I have always believed that if you chase money, you'll never find your dreams. But if you chase your dreams, you'll find the money. I taught school because it was my passion. If it were not, I would have become a full-time agent after I started to represent Rich Campbell. However, after celebrating my 25th anniversary as a teacher, I did decide it was time to move on. I have seen too many teachers burn out—good teachers who lost the spark they had for teaching—and I had been doing it for a long time. Also, after having been an agent throughout the 1980s, my passion for the agency now matched my passion for teaching. I look at it as a job transferal rather than a career change. That's because as the head of a sports agency, I still teach and coach.

Now that I'm approaching age 60, people ask, "When are you going to retire?"

My standard reply is, "Why would I want to retire from a job that most people would die to have?" Lynn and I are having too much fun to retire.

The other ex–history teacher submerged in the world of professional football is Mike Holmgren. He shares my sentiments. "I loved being a teacher," he exclaims. "Today, I still see myself as a teacher, because as a coach, I still have the role of a teacher. I am a very fortunate man because I have been able to put together the two things I love most—teaching and football. It's wonderful to be able to get up in the morning and enjoy your life's work."

Holmgren is an anomaly in professional football. He was a professional educator who got into coaching much later than the norm. I don't know of anyone who has gone from being a professional educator to winning the Super Bowl in such a short time. Remember, he was teaching high school in 1980, and he won the Super Bowl in January 1997.

"I used to go to football coaching clinics," Holmgren tells, "and somebody in the audience would say, 'You were teaching at Oak Grove High School, and eight years later, you were a coordinator with the '49ers. How do you do that? I want to do that.'

"My stock reply has always been, 'I can't tell you, other than I have always been happy wherever I was. Love where you are and work hard where you are, and I can assure you opportunities and good things will come your way.'"

★   ★   ★

MIKE SHERMAN HAS HAD A strong passion for the game of football since his boyhood, tracing back to Northborough, Massachusetts, where he was a three-sport athlete in high school, lettering in football, wrestling, and track. In 1977, he went on to be an offensive lineman and defense end at Central Connecticut State University. He was a solid small-school player, but never good enough to play at a Division I level. He describes himself as a plugger. "I loved the game of football so much—I even loved to practice. I thrived on the challenges, cherishing each success, always the last to leave the locker room after a win. I even appreciated learning from the failures. I placed a high value on the integral bonds and relationships that were built in team sports."

After picking up a diploma in education, Sherman taught English and coached football at Stamford High School in Connecticut. "Once I got a taste of coaching, I knew that's what I'd do for the rest of my life," he tells. His next gig was two years at Worcester (Massachusetts) Academy, and from there, two years as a graduate assistant at the University of Pittsburgh. At Tulane he was an offensive line coach for two years, then an offensive line coach at Holy Cross for three years, followed by a one-year stint as offensive coordinator at the same school. For four years after that, he went back to being an offensive line coach, at Texas A&M. He next spent one year at UCLA as offensive line coach, and then returned to Texas A&M in 1995–96, again, offensive line coach. Finally, in 1997, after being named offensive coordinator at Texas A&M, Sherman broke into the NFL ranks when Holmgren hired him as a tight ends/assistant offensive line coach. He went to Seattle with Holmgren in 1999, signing on as the Seahawks' offensive coordinator and tight ends coach. In 2000, Sherman was named head coach of the Green Bay Packers. He had paid his dues. His 23-year apprenticeship included four years of high school coaching, 16 years at the college level, and three more years of NFL coaching. All told, his family moved 11 times—such is the life of a football head coach.

Still, the Green Bay Packers head coach never lost his passion for the game of football. He was as zealous as he had been in the days he spent plugging away as a Division II college player. Not surprisingly, his passion permeates the Green Bay Packers organization.

All people with passion are not cut from the same mold. For this reason, each person expresses it differently. Andy Reid, for example, has a zeal for football; however, a quiet man, his passion is not as demonstrative as Gruden's or Fox's, two expressive individuals who bubble with enthusiasm. For this reason, people have said to me, "I can envision Jon Gruden, raving and shouting and straining his vocal cords, summoning up every ounce of energy in his body to inspire his players to go into battle with a take-no-prisoners mind-set. But Andy Reid? No, he's too soft-spoken and gentle."

Indeed, Andy Reid comes across like a "Gentle Ben." He truly is one of the most caring, giving men I have ever met, and outwardly, bears little resemblance to a stereotypical head football coach—a Vince Lombardi or a Tom Landry, for instance. But don't be fooled by appearance and think he lacks passion or can't inspire men to play at their uppermost level. His style of leadership doesn't require him to pound his fist on tabletops. He doesn't swear or yell at his players to "get out there and annihilate the opposition!" His win-loss record is a testimony to how effective he is, with his more subtle passion. As Rick Burkholder, the Eagles' head trainer says, "Andy Reid is one of the greatest motivators in the history of the NFL. And I don't think he's ever given a motivational talk."

The fact is, Andy Reid is not an animated guy. He doesn't jump up and down on the sidelines. His passion is a quiet, more subdued exhilaration. Just the same, you know it's there, because you can sense it by his intensity, even though he's calm and methodical. Anyone who knows him knows his passion for his work. As Eagles offensive coordinator Brad Childress says, "Andy has a strong passion for football, and other people can feel that passion because he exudes conviction and confidence. When Andy addresses our team, there's dead quiet in the room. They believe as gospel everything he tells them."

THE CONTRAST BETWEEN AN EAGLES team meeting and one of Jon Gruden's with the Buccaneers is striking. With Gruden it's like you're at a revival. "I'm not in my office all damn day and night to see this bullshit going on out here," Gruden will tell his troops. "We better pick it up. I'm not wasting my time or your time." The players respond to his message. Andy Reid isn't shy about reading the riot act to a player or the entire team, but he never curses. Never. He is a devout Mormon, and while he doesn't criticize swearing, he personally refrains from foul language.

It would be unlikely that a fan in the stands or a television viewer would pick up on Andy Reid's passion for the game of football. What you see from a distance is a large, robust man who appears stoic, even unemotional. Only those close to him—the members of the Philadelphia Eagles organization—know the real Andy Reid. This inner circle know it by his day-in, day-out work ethic, his commitment to his players and coaching staff. With Jon Gruden you can see it by his body language and his facial expressions. There's no hiding it. They're dead giveaways to all in view that he is indeed a very passionate man.

In 2001, *People* magazine voted Gruden one of America's 50 most beautiful people. No doubt, he has leading-man good looks. But it was his sideline facial expressions during a Raiders game in 1998 that earned him his nickname, "Chucky." It happened when running back Harvey Williams was the victim of the head coach's wrath and Gruden tore into him for going the wrong way on an audible. The television audience was privy to a close-up view of the coach's arched eyebrow, his glaring eyes, and a lopsided grin that expressed his chagrin. This startling sight prompted reporters to write about Gruden's striking likeness to devil doll Chucky in the *Child's Play* movies, the creature that goes around killing everybody.

"Williams went to the left when he should have gone right," Gruden explains. "With five major networks televising the game, a newspaper puts a picture of Chucky next to a photo of me in the sports page and the next thing I know, no one knows my name anymore. Soon thousands of fans start taking Chucky dolls to the Raiders games and they're sporting Chucky masks and T-shirts."

The Buccaneers encounter his intensity and passion on a daily basis. They are privy to the countless hours he puts in at One Buccaneers Place. Setting his alarm for 3:17 A.M. every morning, working close to midnight, Gruden gets by on three to four hours sleep each night. At one time, he worried about not getting enough shut-eye. "Why can't I sleep? What's wrong with me?" he asked. He visited several doctors, tried sleeping pills—nothing worked. People had him convinced that it wasn't good for anyone to operate on so little sleep, cautioning him that running on empty was potentially harmful to his health. One doctor asked, "Why do you set your clock for 3:17 every morning? Why not 3:15 or 3:30?" Gruden explained to him that 3:17

was the time set on the alarm when he bought it. "I just never bothered changing it," he said grinning.

After meeting with several doctors over the years, one advised him not to worry about it. "Think of it as a strength. You're blessed because you don't require a lot of sleep. I suggest that you find something you love doing, and you'll have more time to do it—and be better at it." Gruden followed his doctor's advice and he did get better at it. Years later, he was the youngest head coach in NFL history to win a Super Bowl.

Head coaches are notorious for their work ethic, but nobody in the game matches the hours Gruden puts in. That kind of energy can be fueled only by pure passion for his work. Where does such passion come from? Perhaps it's a mix of the right genes and environment. His father, Jim Gruden, was an assistant coach during Jon's youth at the University of Indiana and later at Notre Dame. Jon was 14 years old when the family moved to Bloomington, Indiana, where he got a firsthand view of football head coach Lee Corso, famous for his work habits and inspirational tactics. As a youngster, Jon also became pals with Tim Knight, the son of legendary basketball head coach Bobby Knight. It could be that some of Bobby Knight's intensity rubbed off on him. At the very least, Knight made a lasting impression on the young boy. At age 16, Jim Gruden moved his family to South Bend, Indiana, where he joined Dan Devine's coaching staff. The hallowed grounds of Notre Dame intensified the teenager's passion for football.

Gruden saw how hard his father worked, both with the losing Indiana team and a winning team—Notre Dame. "At Indiana, my dad took some real thrashings from Ohio State," he tells. Later, while still at an impressionable age, he also learned about success when Jim Gruden coached at Notre Dame during the Joe Montana era.

His mother Kathy, a schoolteacher, also had a strong work ethic, arriving at school at 6:45 each morning to get ready for her classes. She worked nights and weekends finding ways to inspire her students. "You have to have a passion for what you do," she told her three sons. "And a quest for excellence within yourself." She referred to it as "self-inflicted pressure." She repeated what her father had told her as she was growing up: "The worst thing you can do in life is go to a job you don't like. Make sure you find your passion."

Kathy and Jim Gruden's love for their work made them wonderful role models for their boys. "I saw how my parents loved what they did and the time and energy they devoted to their professions. Consequently, I know no other way to coach. I tell young people to find something you believe in that you love. When you feel this way, you will succeed."

As the Buccaneers' assistant to head coach/football operations, Mark Arteaga understands the impact Gruden's passion has on those around him. Gruden brought Arteaga with him from Oakland to Tampa Bay; their history of working together dates back to 1998. "I've seen Jon speak in front of the players," Arteaga says, "and if you aren't motivated to play for him, then nothing can motivate you. His passion is so contagious, it kind of spills over. The players know he pours his whole life into it for them, for us, for the organization. He works day and night for us so we will be a champion."

Upon Gruden's arrival, the players didn't exactly roll out a red carpet welcoming him to Tampa Bay. At age 39, he replaced Tony Dungy, a popular head coach with the players, fans, and local media. Although Gruden came to town with a reputation of being an offensive genius, with the huge price tag to acquire him, he was going to have to prove himself. Some of the cool reception Gruden initially received had to do with Tony Dungy's excellent record during his stay. In 1996, Dungy's first year with Tampa Bay, the team went 6-10, but ever since, they were winners, going 47-32 for their next five seasons, playing in six postseason games. It would take less than a heartbeat for a majority of the other NFL teams to swap their five-year records with Tampa Bay's under Dungy's reign. But the Glazers wanted more. Jon Gruden was brought in for a single purpose: to win a Super Bowl.

Although the players and coaching staff cynically viewed their new coach with wariness, it was only a matter of time before Gruden won them over. That's because he not only outworked everyone, he never tired, and he had energy to burn. In time, the players, coaches, and everyone else in the organization—staff personnel, equipment people, and executives—began to push themselves to work harder and do better too. As the saying goes, "The speed of the leader is the speed of the gang."

At first, Warren Sapp, one of the most dominant defensive players in recent times, had a wait-and-see attitude toward the new head coach. It didn't take long, however, for Sapp to warm up to Gruden. The six-two, 303-pound future Hall of Famer says it was Gruden's determination that won his admiration. "He is a madman. He wakes up while I'm rolling over!" the five-time All-Pro tackle says. "It became a challenge the way he poked at us and it became really personal for us. It put us in a whole different mindset."

"He is the consummate salesman," says offensive line coach Bill Muir. "His enthusiasm is contagious. He can sell you like a carnival barker with a $1.25 snake oil bottle that will cure anything."

Oakland Raiders quarterback Rich Gannon raves about his ex-coach: "Of all the coaches I've been around, he's most like a player. He'd give me plays during practice, and often he'd get in the middle of the huddle and call the plays. He'd love to take the snap. Then, in meetings, his comments were comical. I would say ruthless, but with his tone they were just hysterical."

"He's a special guy," says Roland Williams, Oakland Raiders tight end, when speaking of his former head coach. "Not only with the X's and O's, but also because he knows how to get us going, and his love for the game comes through. I'd play for him forever."

LIKE THE OTHER HEAD COACHES, the Carolina Panthers' John Fox has a strong passion for his work. You can hear it when he speaks because he's consumed with enthusiasm. You see his passion in the gleam in his eye. Fox is very likeable. I can't think of anyone I ever met that makes such a good first impression. He has one of those engaging personalities that immediately wins you over because he seems so interested in *you*. No matter that Fox has a hundred different things on his mind, when he looks you in the eye and speaks to you, you feel as though you're the most important person in the world—that's because at the time, to John Fox, you are!

When Fox arrived in Charlotte in 2002, he took over a team that had a 1-15 record, the worst in the NFL. It was his passion for football that convinced everyone—players, coaches, staff members—that the fortunes of the team were destined to change. "I had to get rid of the losing mentality," Fox explains. "I made noticeable changes in personnel so everyone could see that going forward, we'd be a different organization, not the one that lost 15 consecutive games. I carefully brought in people who I knew shared my passion and enthusiasm— people who spend more time with the players than I do. These were people I knew because I had worked with them at other organizations over the years. They were individuals with the same energy level and passion that I have for this game."

One such individual that Fox recruited was Sal Sunseri, a defensive line coach and former All-American linebacker at the University of Pittsburgh in 1981. A remarkable thing about Sunseri's collegiate playing days is he began as a walk-on who became a three-year starter. Following his graduation, Sunseri had been an assistant coach at several colleges, and in the mid-1980s he and Fox worked together with the Pitt Panthers. In 2002, they were reunited once again as "Panthers"—this time in Carolina.

"John Fox really loves his work," tells Sunseri. "He lives, sleeps, and breathes it. This is evidenced by his 'instant recall' with plays going way back to the early days of his career. For instance, he'll say to me, 'Do you remember when we were at Pitt playing Penn State? In the third quarter, they ran such-and-such play on a third and 10.' He can visually picture it, and even recall what defense we were in. Only someone with a real love for football can do that!

"When Foxy first came to Pitt in '86, he was defensive coordinator and secondary coach. He took a defensive unit in the bottom half of the NCAA and completely turned it around. Within three years, it was one of the top 10 defensive teams in the nation. I attribute his success to his passion for his players. He wants so badly for them to succeed. If a player is doing something wrong, John will inform him how to correct it. He'll say it in a forceful yet nonthreatening manner. 'Hey this needs to be done. This is the way I want you to do it. Get it done this way.' He will deal with a specific incident right on the spot. He does this with consistency and everyone feels comfortable with it."

HOLMGREN, SHERMAN, REID, GRUDEN, AND Fox are deeply committed to their life's work. Sure, they express it differently. Some are more demonstrative than others. That's because their love for the game is expressed in a variety of ways. When it comes to having passion, there is no cookie-cutter formula. Nonetheless, it is a common denominator that I believe is required to be a good leader. More than that, it is necessary for a good life.

People sometimes refer to work as "the salt mines" or "the grind." To them, work and drudgery are synonymous. I feel sorry for people with contempt for their work, people who dread getting out of bed each morning. As William Faulkner wrote, "You can't eat for eight hours a day nor drink for eight hours a day, nor make love for eight hours a day—all you can do for eight hours is work. Which is the reason why man makes himself and everybody else so miserable and unhappy."

Passion for our work is what drives us to push ourselves beyond our limits. It energizes us to exert an extra effort, which is often the difference between failure and success, defeat and victory. Here's how it works: Think about a time when you came home after a long day in the workplace. You're absolutely whipped. Then you receive a call from a friend to play a round of tennis or go jogging, and the next thing you know, you're dripping with perspiration, yet filled with a newfound energy. How could it be when you were drop-dead tired after work? The difference is that you're engaged in something you enjoy, that you thrive on. Similarly, men and women who thrive on their work enjoy the advantage of having abundant energy.

As I'm sure you can tell, I feel blessed because I love my work. I can't wait to begin my day every morning. This attitude stays with me throughout the day and provides added stamina to keep me going at full speed. I felt the same way when I taught at school. I believe my enthusiasm inspired my students to learn about history. I could tell by the way they participated in class, did their homework, and excelled on their examinations. Besides, there was always a high demand to enroll in my courses. The word spread throughout the campus that "LaMonte's history lectures are exciting and interesting. Sign up for his classes."

Unfortunately, exciting is not a word we hear enough of when young people talk about studying history. That's because there are teachers who dread teaching it. They fall into that category of people that get up and go to a job they can't stand. Their negative attitudes carry over to their students. Just as enthusiasm is contagious, so is monotony. A teacher with passion can make any subject exciting, whether it's science, math, or literature—any subject. It's the teacher's job to excite his or her students.

Imagine the positive impact a parent's passion for his or her work has on a child. When you leave the house each morning filled with enthusiasm for your job, you send a positive signal to your child that work is a joy. Conversely, if you dread going to work each morning and complain about your day at the dinner table, this is also picked up by your kids. What a terrible legacy to pass on to them! When our son Brian decided to major in history at San Jose State University, I felt blessed, knowing that my passion had rubbed off on him.

Having passion for one's work is important in all fields. I've seen it firsthand in my work as a teacher, coach, and salesman. A salesman who doesn't think his product is the best thing since sliced bread won't close many sales. I can't tell you how many times I was "just shopping" for a new car, suit, or television set, and an enthusiastic salesman talked me into a purchase. Did you ever accept a free two- or three-day trip to a time-sharing resort where your only obligation for the vacation was that you had to listen to a mandatory sales presentation? I know many people who went only because it was a "free-bie" and vowed they'd never buy a time-share unit. But they did. The companies that make these offers know what they're doing. They know that many people will change their minds and buy a unit once they're in front of an enthusiastic salesperson. They know how contagious enthusiasm is—and how it loosens otherwise tight purse strings.

Recruiters of well-run companies pay close attention to the passion exhibited by job interviewees. I know business leaders who prioritize it. "People can be taught how to do their work," a top executive told me, "but we can't teach passion, so we seek people who already have it." He went on to emphasize that if there was a choice between hiring one of two job candidates, he'd hire the one with the most passion over a slightly more qualified person. "We have a lot of passionate people who work here," he said, "and we seek out the individual who will adapt to our company's culture. Someone who lacks passion won't fit in around here."

Of course, while looking for people with passion, it's important to understand that not everybody exhibits it the same way. As with coaches, some people ooze with so much enthusiasm that they are about to burst. But then other people don't show it because they are more inhibited. Don't overlook the undemonstrative ones. Not everyone reacts the same way when they're turned on. There are quiet, reserved people in this world who are also equally driven to succeed. By asking thoughtful questions about their interests—and then being a good listener, those with passion will reveal it. Sometimes, you just have to do some digging. For example, if he's a fly fisherman, talk about fly fishing; if he's a gourmet cook, talk about cooking, and so on. Hit on the right subject and they won't be able to conceal their animation.

Where does passion start within an organization? Any organization, whether it be a football team, a government agency, a business enterprise? It starts with the leader—the guy at the top—and permeates throughout the organization. People feel it in the hall-ways, in the warehouses, everywhere. Visitors in the building feel it too. Passion spreads like wildfire internally and then externally to vendors and customers.

3

The Trust Factor

"Trust men and they will be true to you; trust them greatly and they will show themselves great."

—RALPH WALDO EMERSON

By mid-November in Minnesota, the early morning temperature drops below freezing, and Sunday, November 17, 2002, was no exception. After two winters in Green Bay, the cold weather didn't stop Mike Sherman from taking a brisk walk in downtown Minneapolis. The Packers' head coach wanted some quiet time by himself before the Packers-Vikings game that afternoon. Having won seven consecutive games and 8-1 for the season, Sherman was thinking, "Life is good."

On his way back to the hotel, he passed a homeless man. Without hesitation, Sherman approached him and handed him a few dollars.

"Here, take this," the head coach said, and then he added, "I'm headed for my hotel. How about coming with me? I'll treat you to a good breakfast."

The two men went back to the hotel and went to Sherman's suite and ordered room service. "While we're waiting you're welcome to take a hot shower," he said.

The man cleaned up and ate a hearty breakfast. "I'm sorry but I've got to go to the stadium," Sherman apologized. On his way out the door, he added, "Say, would you like to go to today's game?"

The man's face lighted up. "Yes, I would."

"Great!" Sherman said. "I'll have my security man drive you to the stadium. I'll have a pass for him to pick up for you. You'll be on the field. On sidelines with the team, that is, if you don't mind being on the Packers' side."

Throughout the afternoon, the homeless man kept saying, "I can't believe this is happening to me. I must be dreaming."

This kind gesture was Sherman's way to express his thankfulness for his blessings. When I heard about it, I questioned him, "Weren't you concerned about taking a homeless person to your hotel room? A complete stranger?"

"I would be more concerned if I didn't help him," answered Sherman. "I'm realistic enough to realize that the only difference between myself and that homeless gentleman may have just been opportunity. I got one and he didn't. It's that simple. And that opportunity that I got does not mean I'm a better man than he."

Another of my favorite stories about Sherman's benevolence involved a teenage boy who was abandoned by his parents at birth. The boy lived in a halfway house for orphans in the Green Bay area. Born with severe respiratory complications, he had to breathe with a ventilator. His poor condition kept him house-confined for nearly three years. An avid Packers fan, the boy's biggest dream was to meet Coach Sherman. When Mike heard this, he quietly visited the boy and stayed for an entire afternoon. Mike has continued to keep in touch with him ever since that first meeting.

Then there was the time when Mike, Karen, and their four children were about to embark on a family vacation. En route to their destination, the family went via Milwaukee, where they stopped at a cancer ward. They spent several hours visiting and cheering up patients. This to Sherman was a reality check. "Karen and I think it's important for our family to realize how blessed we were, and no matter how much we have, it should never be taken for granted." It is not idle words when Coach Sherman says, "My faith, my family, and the Green Bay Packers are the most important things in my life."

All members of the Green Bay Packers organization know that their head coach has a burning desire to win the Super Bowl. His passion and competitive spirit are readily apparent. "I want to go to the Super Bowl and win it in the worst way," he tells the team, "but I am not going to lose my family in the process. That's not a trade I am willing to make. Nor is it one I would ask any of you to make." He reminds the players that their priorities should be: "God first, family second, career third." Without hesitation, he adds: "I think having career in the number three spot is high enough that if we all keep it number three, we can get done what we need to get done. But third place is high enough and should never come before God and family. I just don't want any of you letting it slip further down your list of priorities."

You may be thinking, What does a story about Mike Sherman's kindness to a homeless man, a visit to see a sick boy, or a family visit to a cancer clinic have to do with leadership? My answer: Everything!

That's because leadership is based on trust. To quote Ralph Waldo Emerson: "What you do speaks so loudly that I cannot hear what you say." Coach Sherman's actions speak about the kind of man he is. His actions spawn trust.

How could you *not* trust this man? The fact is, the people around Mike Sherman trust him unconditionally. And trust is the foundation upon which good leadership is built. Without trust, one cannot lead.

"In order for people to follow you," articulates Sherman, "you must be a person of high integrity. With integrity, there is belief. Having people believe in you directly affects leadership. This also requires being brutally honest with others as well as yourself. This means telling people what you are going to do—and doing it. This gives a leader the right to make demands on people. It can't be that don't-do-as-I-do-but-as-I-say-you-do bull. Such behavior destroys credibility. What's more, don't be slow in admitting when you are wrong. You gain people's trust when you admit making a mistake. This too is integrity. When I make a mistake, I'm the first to admit it, and I'll simply say to the team, 'I was wrong, and hopefully what I did can serve as a lesson and we can learn from it.' When you are wrong, the worst thing you can do is cover up for it. Generally, the longer the period that expires before you admit your wrongdoings, the more trouble you get yourself into.

"Whenever I see a player or coach who does something wrong, I am quick to confront him. If I see a player or coach do something well, I also confront him with positive reinforcement. This can only be done in an organization that fosters openness among its people. In the wrong environment, people will build barriers and act defensively. I'm constantly telling our people, 'In order for us to be successful, each of us must be able to handle the truth. When something is wrong, it is wrong. When something is right, it is right. We have to know the difference.' This is a prerequisite in order for us to be a great organization. We must be able to accept the truth—even when the truth hurts. Each of us must be able to accept the cold facts of reality that when something is not right, you better get it fixed or somebody else will be fixing it instead of you.'

"People have to know that you shoot straight with them," Sherman continues. "They come to expect the truth even though they may not want to hear it. They *think* they don't, but deep down, I believe they really do. They want you to be straight with them and know you won't BS them. In a healthy atmosphere, people should be able to say, 'I know if I ask him where I stand, he'll tell me.' "

It works both ways with Mike Sherman. If you tell him you'll do something, you better do it. "At the last minicamp," he recalls, "I met with a group of some of our very large-sized players. I posed the question to the group: 'How much are you going to weigh when you come back?'

"They started to throw numbers out. A 380-pound offensive lineman, for example, yelled out, 'I'll be back weighing 350 pounds,' and another said, 'I'm going to lose 40 pounds.' Sometimes, they get carried away and make a commitment in front of the other players that will be hard to keep.

"If a player says, 'One pound,' I can handle it. But I don't want anyone telling me something that he can't deliver on. 'Be honest with your teammates and your coach,' I harp at them.

"It's probable if a player commits to a very low number I'll say, 'You need to do more than that.' But I'll respect him for saying it. What I don't want to hear is somebody mouthing off about how he's going to lose 20 or 40 pounds and come back having lost only two pounds, or worse, actually putting on some extra weight. If he tells me something, he better do it. I will hold him accountable to what he commits to do."

★ ★ ★

AFTER MIKE HOLMGREN COACHED HIS last game with Green Bay, losing in a playoff game to the '49ers by a score of 23-10, he was invited for a job interview with the Seattle Seahawks. The Seahawks made him an offer he couldn't refuse.

Bill Nayes, who has the title of football operations team coordinator/team travel with the Seahawks, had been working for the Packers at the time. Nayes recalls a conversation with Holmgren: "Coach Holmgren said to me, 'I'm going to Seattle and would like you to come with me. Are you interested?'

" 'Count me in.' I replied without hesitation.

"Once the word was out that Holmgren was leaving, several others met with him to discuss going with him. Mike told us to start moving our families to Seattle, and that's exactly what we all did. Meanwhile, we had no contracts with Seattle, nor did any of us know what our salaries would be. Until then, I had lived in Wisconsin all of my life, so a relocation to Seattle was a big move for me. I'm sure it was to all the guys, particularly the ones with large families who had already settled in Green Bay. Housing costs in Seattle are considerably higher than in Green Bay. In fact, it's not even close. Everything costs more out here. The reason why we were all willing to make the move was because we had so much faith in Mike. He's our leader and we trust him. It's as simple as that. Whatever he'd ask any of us to do, we'd do it, knowing that he's going to look out for us—and do what's in our best interest. A total of ten of us that included coaches, trainers, and administrative staff went with him. Nobody even asked questions. That's the kind of faith we had in Mike. The only thing he told us before the move was that he was given a long-term contract, so we did have the security in knowing that we'd be in Seattle for several years.

"When I go back home," Nayes continues, "my friends call me a traitor. They say, 'How could somebody from Wisconsin ever leave the Green Bay Packers? Man, you had the greatest job in the world.'

" 'I did it,' I tell them, 'because of Coach Holmgren.' I had so much confidence in him, and he's the guy I work for. This is what he looks for in people. You have to work your butt off for him, but you always know he's going to take care of you."

I know exactly what Bill Nayes means because I've known Mike Holmgren for a long time, and you'll never meet a more straightforward guy. Everyone knows he'll always be truthful with them, and he often says, "Look, if you ask me a question, make sure you want to know the answer." One thing is certain—he will let you know where you stand with him. Sometimes you might not like the answer he gives you, but he'll be honest with you. I've never known him to tell a lie. For instance, if a player says, "Coach, why aren't I starting?" he'll give him specific reasons. If a player asks why he got cut, he'll tell him exactly why. He doesn't mince words. He doesn't do it in a harsh way, and it's not personal. The bottom line is that the players respect him because he will tell the truth.

For instance, Seattle recruited a wide receiver who was a free agent and had been released from Chicago. He wasn't a high-priced free agent, nor was he a player that other teams were clamoring to recruit. But the Seahawks wanted him, believing he could fill a role for the team. This player didn't think his previous head coach leveled with him, and he was unhappy with the direction his career was going. Before he signed with Seattle, Mike didn't pull any punches with him. "Look, we want you here. We have a role for you on our team, but you are not going to be a starter. We have two young players that we plan on giving every opportunity to be the starters. Now if one of them gets hurt, or he can't do it, then yes, absolutely, you'll get an opportunity to start. But I'm not going to tell you what you want to hear so you'll sign."

Some head coaches will say anything to get a player to sign and then they'll deal with it later. Mike doesn't operate like that. This player respected his truthfulness and he signed a one-year contract with Seattle. As it turned out, he was the team's third wide receiver and did start in some games with formations that required three wide receivers. When his contract was up, he signed on again, and he has played a significant role on the team. This is his third year with the team."

As Holmgren explains, "I never lied to a player or a coach—not even to the press. My philosophy is that honesty has to permeate your entire existence. You must live your life this way, at the office and away from the office. This is where you start because if you lose trust, you can't teach. You can't communicate. Your people won't listen to you and you'll never be able to get them to do what needs to be done.

"I place a high premium on honesty and loyalty. I have a standard speech I make to my new coaches at my staff meeting at the beginning of the year. I tell them, 'I hired you, and I make a commitment to you and your family. And you must make a commitment to me. As coaches, we're going to have some bumps in the road along the way, and I will help you through them. But the one thing I will not tolerate is disloyalty. I will be loyal to you and I expect the same thing from you.'"

Gil Haskell signed on as offensive coordinator with the Seahawks in 2000. His friendship with Holmgren goes back to when they were both high school coaches in San Francisco in the late 1970s and competed against each other. Even though they were rivals, they became very good friends and frequently met with a group of other high school coaches in the same league for a 7:30 breakfast on Saturday mornings following Friday night games. "I can say this about Mike," Haskell tells, "he's the same person on and off the field. He's the same guy all the time. What I like about him is that when he's upset, you know he's upset because he'll let you know it. Then you can move on. He won't pull the rug from underneath you and then you can't function. He'll let you know because he'll say, 'Jack, you didn't play very well and this is what you did wrong. I want that to get better.' "

WHEN ANDY REID FIRST TOOK over as the Eagles' head coach in early 1999, one of the first things he did was interview several players because he wanted to get "a feel of the team's pulse." He kept hearing complaints about the team's medical care. Resolved to find a solution and only three weeks on the job, Reid hired Rick Burkholder to be his head trainer. Burkholder had spent the previous six years as the Pittsburgh Steelers' assistant athletic trainer and was considered one of the best trainers in professional sports.

Burkholder recalls an early conversation with his new boss: "Most head coaches would have said, 'You're getting paid a six-figure salary, so I expect you to figure this thing out and come back with some answers.' But that's not Coach Reid's style. He took me in front of all the players at a team meeting and said, 'Fellas, I've talked to many of you, and I've been hearing that you're unhappy with your medical care. I went out and found the best guy possible to straighten this thing out. All that I ask of you guys is that you cooperate with Rick, and in return, he will give you the best medical care in the National Football League. Do this and we'll be alright.'

"Then Coach Reid gave me 45 minutes to explain my program and the changes we planned to make. After I gave my presentation, he stood in front of the team and gave me some more praise. Then he said to everyone, 'Rick is going to do a terrific job. Now if any of you defies him, I'm going to cut your balls off.'

"From my viewpoint, the players are my customers," Burkholder continues, "and he took my customers and gave me an endorsement that set the stage so I couldn't help but succeed. He's telling them how wonderful I am, and raving about everything I'm going to do for them. With everyone giving me his support, he made my job easy. That's Andy Reid. He goes to great lengths to make you look good. He makes everybody in the organization look good.

"I had a conversation with Coach Reid at the beginning of summer camp in '99," recalls Burkholder. "He said to me, 'Rick, I don't care if we win a game this year.'

" 'Coach, your job is based on wins and losses,' I answered.

" 'All that I want is our guys to do the right thing. I want them to hustle. I want them to be on time. I want them to be good character guys. I want them to get better. I want them to be coachable. I want them to cooperate with you. I want them to cooperate with public relations. We'll win games if they do that.'

"I never heard a head coach talk like this before, and I'm like, 'Are you sure about this?'

" 'I'm as competitive as they come,' Coach Reid reminded me. 'I want to win. But this year, I want to do things right first.'

"It took us a while to win our first game. We dropped the first four before we had a W. I was impressed with his sincerity in wanting to do the right thing. After those many private conversations we had, I knew he believed that. I knew where his values were. And I have a feeling that I'm not the only guy he said that to.

"Once we started summer camp and the season was under way, I became even more convinced that he meant what he said. I've been around other head coaches who get boiling mad at the trainer when a player is hurt. They want the trainer to get the injured player back into the game, and some coaches shout, 'We can't win without him. I need that guy. Get him better for Sunday's game.'

"Andy Reid has never been like that. Instead he says, 'I want you to make sure those guys are on time and make them work hard when they're in the training room.' Coach never focuses on the product. He focuses on the process.

"He says, 'Rick, if they're on time, disciplined in your training room, and work hard, they will recover from their injury sooner. However, if they're always late and lazy, it's going to take forever. Injury is a part of the game. I'm not worried that they're hurt.'

"If I don't think a player is going to practice during the week, I'll tell him, 'You probably won't have him on Sunday.'

"If he thinks I'm being a little soft, he'll say, 'If you're as good as I think you are, you'll have him back.' And that's the end of it. He's so gentle that way. The players see this side of him too, and when they're injured, they want to get well quickly so they can play for him."

Burkholder's admiration for Reid is apparent. He knows how competitive his boss is, but also understands that winning isn't everything to him. "Coach Reid worries about the day-to-day business," explains Burkholder. "He expects the same work ethic on the practice field, in the weight room, everywhere. I attend every team meeting because I don't want to miss anything, and I can't recall him ever telling the team anything about winning the upcoming game. What he will say is, 'Okay, today is Wednesday, and here's what we have to focus on.' Then he might say, 'You'll notice on film that this team is very fast and we've got to be crisp in practice.' On Thursday, he might say, 'Today, we are in the red zone. We've got to do this and this and this.' But he never talks about winning the game.

"The night before the game, Coach Reid will say, 'Hey, you guys worked your butts off this week. You've done the right things. Now what you've got to do tomorrow is go out there and let your personality show. Have fun.' He doesn't talk about winning because he doesn't have to. He talks about the things that lead up to winning. That's why he's so successful."

Brad Childress, Philadelphia's offensive coordinator, concurs with Burkholder on Andy Reid's strong emphasis regarding character. "Andy is not seduced by a player's athleticism if he's a bad character person. In today's NFL, it takes strong discipline to think this way. Another head coach might envision a highly talented player as a great receiver or running back, but Andy will have a vision of somebody who will be a good person, an outstanding citizen, and a good fit into our way of doing business. When it comes to character, he'll pass on a star player with a bad attitude. He'd rather take a guy with a bit less talent but with character. He's a believer in the maxim that one bad apple can spoil the barrel. It only takes one guy on the team who's always complaining to bring down a bunch of other guys."

Burkholder recalls being told by Reid: " 'I want good ballplayers and tough guys, but I also want quality guys.' Then he explained, 'I'll tell you why. When the chips are down, the quality guy is always there for you because he'll play his heart out for you.' And that's the kind of guys he looked for, and that's the kind of guys we've got. He wants players that will stick together when the going gets tough. In a team huddle on the sidelines during a game, Coach Reid will tell the players, 'Okay guys, you have to look after one another now.' "

A religious man, Reid believes in practicing his religion throughout the week, not only on Sunday mornings in church. Still, according to Childress, Reid has a speech he gives to the coaching staff every year. "He tells us, 'I want guys with a strong faith, but I don't want you to force it on anybody. There have been wars fought over religion, women, and money. So remember not to force your religion on anybody. Please give them some space."

Most telling about the trust Andy Reid generates is the way he lives. "I try to live by what our church tells us," Reid explains. "Any time I'm not doing football, I am probably going to be with my wife and children. I live by two rules. Number one is to be a good person, and number two is to be honest in my dealings with people. I try to be the same during the good and the bad times. You can't change during the tough times. You can't suddenly be a different person or present things differently to your people. You've got to stay consistent. Stick to your convictions. When players see you have that conviction and stick to them in spite of a lot of criticism, it makes them believe in you too.

"It's easy to be honest with a person when he's doing a good job," Reid continues, "but it's not as easy when he's doing a bad job. For example, you might have a great person but he's not quite good enough to make the football team. There are times when I must release a player who has a family to feed. I have to be honest with him. That's where we started with this team. I was consistent in always shooting straight with everyone. I didn't waiver from this. During the first year with the team, we had our share of highs and lows, but I didn't change. You've got to be consistent, and when you are, your people feel comfortable because they know what to expect."

While it's true that Reid is one of the hardest working persons you'll ever meet, his family comes first. They are still telling stories in Green Bay about how Reid arrived at work at 4:30 in the morning. Then at 7:00, he would go home to pick up his children, drive them to school, and be back at the office by 7:30. Because Green Bay is a small town, it was possible to do that. It isn't possible in Philadelphia because the Reids live too far away from the stadium. During the off-season, he'll slip away from the office to watch one of his sons play football or one of his daughters in a school concert.

It doesn't seem to matter who you talk to about Andy Reid. The people who know him will describe him as an honest and caring man, two important leadership qualities. The fans sense it too. At a summer camp in Bethlehem, Pennsylvania, I saw why they find him so endearing. After the last day of practice, Reid had the entire team stand and, facing the audience, the players applauded the fans. Then they walked among the fans, shaking hands, giving high fives, and signing autographs. This is the positive influence Andy Reid has on the team. He's their leader and because he cares, they care.

COMING TO A TEAM THAT lost its last 15 consecutive games is a grueling task for a seasoned NFL head coach, let alone a rookie coach. When John Fox came to Carolina in 2002, he directly addressed the fact that the team's confidence and morale were low. "I wanted to let them know that they could be winners if they were willing to pay the price," he explains. " 'The same people that say you're a piece of crap when you lose,' I told them, 'will tell you that you're the greatest when you win. It's all based on your performance on Sunday. Well, that's not reality. Reality is the hard work and preparation that go into Sunday's game. And sometimes it's not about winning because success isn't just winning. It's giving your best and being your best all the time. Be the same guy every day.'

"I let them know that winning isn't just what happens on the football field," Fox continues. "A lot of the off-the-field things are involved. That's why there's a big building in New York filled with NFL personnel that monitor everything we do. They have all kinds of drug tests and other evaluations. They're even concerned about the way we invest our money. They're monitoring what you do so you live with character, not characters. We can have a whole bunch of talented individuals, but without the right kind of people, we're not going to be successful in this League. I believe if each of us can be successful in all facets of his life, eventually we will win.

" 'Discipline in your life doesn't just occur while you're here,' I emphasize. 'It occurs in your relationships with your family and social life. To maximize your talents, you have to have discipline in your life. When I talk to you about being smart, I'm not just talking about knowing your plays. I'm talking about how you conduct yourself in life. There's right and there's wrong. We all know what's right and what's wrong. Now are any of us perfect? No. We are going to make mistakes. But we are going to have to pay the price for those mistakes and we are all dependable and accountable to each other.' "

"When Coach Fox stood up in front of the team," explains Sal Sunseri, defensive lineman coach, "they knew he was a guy who had been to The Show. He had been the New York Giants' defensive coordinator in Super Bowl XXXV on January 28, 2001. Although Baltimore defeated New York, 34-7, Fox was recognized as one of the NFL's best defensive coordinators. John had earned his stripes and spoke with authority when he said, 'You can watch the tape on guys in the Super Bowl and you will say that they weren't the most talented group of players, but they were there and there's a reason.' John took guys that weren't really great and he made them great."

New York's defensive lineman Michael Strahan, who set an NFL record with 22.5 sacks in 2001 has high praises for Fox. Strahan said, "I didn't make my career what it has turned out to be until Coach Fox came along. He truly taught me and taught us about football and not just lining up and using your athletic ability to make a play. He took guys that maybe weren't as athletic and made us all understand the game so we could play it faster and play it better." He made Strahan a great football player.

"Fox was a guy who had been to the Show, and he came here as a respected coach," Sal Sunseri continues. "John knows his people, and he knows what he can get out of each player. He knows a player's deficiencies and his strengths. He puts them in a position where the best players make plays and he will help his players that can't. John won't tell you anything that he doesn't believe, hasn't experienced, and hasn't lived through. When he believes that we've got to run the ball to be successful, we are going to run the ball. If he believes we have to stay here longer to watch film, that's what we'll do. Whatever he thinks it takes for us to be our best, he'll make sure we do it. When he tells us something, his conviction comes through, and you know it's how he feels. It's not going to be what he thinks you want to hear."

Sunseri respects Fox because he is realistic and tells it like it is. "I remember when I was coaching with Foxy at the University of Pittsburgh, and we were playing at home against Miami in 1986. It was Vinny Testaverde's senior year when he won the Heisman Trophy and went number one in the draft. Wide receiver Michael Irvin was on the same team and the Cowboys' number one draft choice the following year. Testaverde came out on the first play, drops back five steps and runs eight yards out, and before Irvin even broke out, the ball was there for him to make the catch. I was standing next to Foxy and he looked at me, scratched his head, and said, 'We could stay here all night. There's no way we're stopping that!' We played very tough but got whipped 37-10. That's the way he is. Very realistic.

"John is constantly preaching work ethic. The other day he said to the team, 'When I'm out on the practice range, boy I hit that ball beautiful. But when I step up to the tee, I don't hit it the same way. I want the same guy to put that ball out there whether he's on the practice range or hitting off the tee.' You can see where he's coming from. He tells us that if we want a chance to win, we've got to pay the price. It's preparation that wins games. If you prepare, you're mentally tough, and you're ready, you'll produce. He's very consistent, and during his first season with the Panthers, he kept showing the team what they did well and what they did poorly. Then he let them know why we didn't get it done. 'This is what needs to get done,' he'd say, 'and it always comes down to preparation, people making plays, taking care of it.' He repeats over and over, 'There are two things you can do with pressure. You can either feel it, or you can apply it.' Then it's more practice and still more practice, so when it comes to Sunday, they can do the same thing they practiced all week.

" 'When you put in the time and you invest something into it,' he says, 'you're going to reap the benefits. It's never easy. And sometimes you have to slight your family at home because you're so demanding on yourself, but down the road, you'll reap the benefits with what you can give them.' John is not going to cheat his football team in any way through lack of preparation. If he believes it takes being here at 6:00 A.M. and staying to 2:00 the next morning, he's going to do it.

" 'It's a production world,' John is fond of saying. 'And those who produce will succeed. And those who don't produce are going to fall on their face. It always goes back to preparation. You can't show up for practice and neglect the little things, like taping yourself, watching the film, or having your mind on some other business. You've got to come in here and get your work done, focusing on what you have to do. Staying focused in football is not easy because there are always distractions. But if you come in and prepare your task at hand, then you'll be ready to go.'"

"I always tell them that it's hard to succeed in this League without having a passion for it," asserts Fox. "It's not about fame, nor is it about money. It's what kind of man you are. To me, this means having discipline in all facets of your life. If something is not right in one area of your life, it carries over to other areas. Some people claim they can hide a problem, but it eventually impacts their work, whether it's a drug problem, an alcohol problem, gambling, whatever. 'This is a very short-lived career,' I tell them. 'It doesn't last very long. It's *four for 40*. What you do for the next four years will determine what you do for the next 40 years. You can screw around and do all kinds of crazy shit. And yes, you'll have a good time, but because you goofed up, it will mean you'll have to bust your ass for the next 40 years. Now if you really attack these four years and invest and commit yourself to them, you'll be rewarded for those next 40 years. Remember now, football is a young man's game, so I'm talking about longevity. Be smart so you won't regret it later on.' It's a simple lesson to comprehend. You're going to get out of it what you put in. But it's more than simply having the talent. You must have the discipline."

WHEN JON GRUDEN WAS HIRED by Tampa Bay, he replaced Tony Dungy, who was admired by both players and Buccaneers fans alike. During his six-year tenure with Tampa Bay, Dungy had amassed a respectable 54-42 record that included four playoff games. Prior to his arrival, the Buccaneers had finished in last place in their division for three consecutive years. Dungy, one of four African-American head coaches in the

NFL, is credited with having built Tampa Bay's strong defensive unit, which was number one in its division while he was at the helm. Replacing such a respectable and accomplished coach posed a real challenge to Jon Gruden.

"At the first team meeting," Gruden reminisces, "I acknowledged that I understood there was controversy over my coming to Tampa. 'Tony Dungy is a great coach and a great man,' I said. 'You guys did a heck of a job under him. I respect the job Tony did. Now it's our job to finish the hard work that you guys have done to put yourselves on the brink of being a great team. I don't know how I got here, but I am here, and I want you to give me a chance. Give me the opportunity to implement my program here. I need your help.'

"Throughout the season and to this day, we acknowledge Coach Dungy and what he meant to this franchise," says Gruden. "I appealed to the leaders on the team for this help, who are among the best players in football. You don't just walk in and start calling plays, implementing schedules, and get everyone's immediate respect. You have to earn that. And hard work and everyday consistency is something I do so I can get it."

The game of football is built on trust. Players must trust their coaches and their trainers. They must believe they are prepared to perform at their peak. Likewise, the players must trust each other. Every player must trust each of his 10 teammates on the field to do his job. If one man doesn't—someone misses a block, a receiver runs a wrong route—a busted play results. It could be a blocked kick, a fumble, an intercepted pass. This is why football is such a great team sport. As the adage goes, a chain is only as strong as its weakest link. If a player doesn't trust the guy next to him to do his job and tries to compensate by covering for him, then his own assignment is left undone.

"If you want to earn a person's trust—and this doesn't just apply to football, I could be talking about earning your spouse's trust or a coworker's trust—you've got to be there for them when they hit that bump in the road," Gruden explains. "When the quarterback throws an interception, a head coach can't go crazy, change the game plan, and call a run every play. You've got to help bring him back. You've got to be there for people when things get tough. Now if things are always tough, you're probably not any good or you're going to have to make some changes. And you've got to be consistent. You can't be a good guy after a win and be crazy-out-of-your-mind when you have a bad first half or lose a game. You've got to give these guys some consistency."

Based on my personal observations, all NFL head coaches have a good work ethic. But throughout the sports world, everyone marvels at Jon Gruden, who puts in 16- to 18-hour days. Jon calls it, "grinding," and when he calls you a "grinder," you should take it as a compliment. Gruden's strong work ethic has permeated the entire Tampa Bay organization, and its consequence has resulted in a high level of trust. As Gruden puts it, "It's one thing to deliver a corny rah-rah speech, but quite another when you see 15 or 16 of our coaches in here on their day off. And these same guys are doing their homework in the evenings when they are not here. The players see this and know their coaches are grinding away to give them a chance to win and excel. It makes the players want to come in here and execute to the utmost of their abilities. They understand that there is going to be pressure on them to excel. It's applied pressure. 'Apply the pressure,' I tell them. 'Don't feel it, apply it.' That's what we want here. To do it, you've got to execute."

Garrett Giemont, the Buccaneers' strength and conditioning trainer, says, "Gruden's the leader pulling everyone on that rope, inch by inch, continually trying to make you better, and at the same time, making you want to be better. It's like a kid who pushes himself in school because he doesn't want to disappoint his parents. We see the genuine love Jon has for his work, and it makes you want to bust your ass because when you see his face, you don't want to let him down. Why? Because you know he's not letting you down. How can you *not* trust a guy like this?"

On Sunday, November 17, 2002, Green Bay was playing in Tampa Bay in a close game tied at 7-7 with 7:33 remaining in the third quarter. Both teams were strong contenders to win their division. Brett Favre was trying to connect with Terry Glenn on a post pattern; however, the Buccaneers' secondary had the wide receiver double-covered with strong safety John Lynch deep, and cornerback Brian Kelly made the pick. Kelly made a 31-yard return that set up the go-ahead touchdown. During the play, the Bucs' Warren Sapp plowed into the Packers' offensive tackle Chad Clifton. The game was delayed for several minutes while Clifton was strapped to a backboard and hauled off the field. Clifton lost feeling in his extremities for a brief period. The in-stadium video screens showed a zoomed-in view of the injured player as he lay motionless; also picked up by the camera was Sapp doing a celebration dance. No penalty was called.

Tampa won the game, 21-7. After the last play, Mike Sherman walked over to the other side of the field to congratulate Gruden. Upon crossing paths with Warren Sapp, Sherman simply couldn't restrain himself and accused him of taking a cheap shot at one of his players. Sherman's remarks resulted in a heated argument and triggered an incident that received more media coverage than the game itself. Several weeks had passed when I discussed the brouhaha with several members of the Green Bay organization. Each expressed how proud he was that their 48-year-old head coach had stood eyeball-to-eyeball with the 303-pound, All-Pro Warren Sapp, to protect a Packers player. It's probable that Sapp's hit was in the heat of the game and there was no malicious intent to injure Chad Clifton. Likewise, Sherman's reaction was a spontaneous expression of his passion for the game and his strong loyalty to his players, who thought his action spoke volumes. It demonstrated that they had a leader who would lead them into battle and would never abandon them.

When Donald Driver signed a long-term contract with the Packers, the All-Pro wide receiver's voice cracked and tears streamed down his face when he expressed how happy he was to be part of the Green Bay Packers organization. "I can't tell you how much I appreciate Coach Sherman and everybody in this organization," Driver said. It's a two-way street. Mike Sherman expects a lot from his players, and in turn, they expect a lot from him. This is a special relationship built on trust.

Trust isn't earned in a single big swoop. For the most part, it is earned by a series of little things, many of which are seemingly insignificant, but in total, have a lasting impact. For instance, it could be Mike Sherman inviting the players' families to a scrimmage at the stadium that's followed by a barbeque. Or it could be John Fox inviting the coaches and players with their wives to a dinner dance. Or Andy Reid inviting the coaches' and players' families to visit summer training camp in Bethlehem, Pennsylvania, a small town 40 miles north of Philadelphia, and taking them out to dinner. However thoughtful, it takes a lot more to inspire trust in people. It is earned by your everyday actions, little by little. It takes time for a leader to know his people, and for them to know him.

"I know what they're like on the field," John Fox explains. "I'm interested in knowing what they're like in a different setting. At a social gathering, I can meet their spouses. I want to get to know Karl

Hankton's wife, Jennifer, and Muhsin Muhammad's wife, Christa. I know that I'm never going to get to know them if I don't see them. To me, it's a way to show our people that I really do care about them, not only professionally."

"We've been known to call off a practice and take everyone to bowling or to a movie," says Gruden. "It's great being together. Having fun. Sitting next to each other and having popcorn. It can't be all business all the time. Maybe it's a round of golf now and then. For instance, I'm talking golf with Warren Sapp and Anthony McFarland, and I say, 'You guys think you know a thing about golf? Let's go out and let's settle this thing right now.' It's good to get away from business. Even when we travel, it's fun to get on the airplane with our players because I enjoy their company. I feel as if I could sit down and have a private conversation with any one of them. I hope they all feel the same way about me. If I feel like I've gotten the jaundiced eye from someone, I'm going to confront him about it. If there's a problem, I want to how we can improve the relationship. I demand a lot from our players, and I want them to demand a lot from me in return."

The people that work for you must know that your interest in them is not profit-motivated. You can't treat them as if they are a piece of income-producing machinery. They have to know it's more personal if you want to win their trust and loyalty. It's the little gestures you do that people pick up on that lets them know you care. Carol Wilson, Andy Reid's assistant, reveals how this works when she talks about her boss. "In the middle of the season, Andy had a million things on his mind, and yet he noticed that my eyes were all teary when I came to work one day. 'Are you okay, Carol?' he asked. 'Yes, I'm fine,' I said. A little while later, he asked the same question, and again I said I was okay. Later, I was in his office and told him I needed to take a break so I could take some allergy pills. 'Ah, that's it,' he said. 'I didn't know if you were crying or whatever. I was worried about you, Carol.' I was touched because he cared about how I felt. Andy's the kind of person who truly cares when he stops to talk to someone and asks, 'How you doing?'"

When television viewers see Andy Reid on the sidelines on a Sunday afternoon, they perceive a hard-nosed football coach with ice water running through his veins. Yes, that's Andy Reid. But what they don't see is another side, a man who is a gentle, caring family man. This is also Andy Reid, the same father of daughter, Crosby, who, when she was 14 years old, sang the National Anthem at Veterans Stadium in front of a full house of 68,000. Prior to game time, head of security Butch Buchanico walked with Andy through the stadium tunnel leading to the playing field. "I've seen him face the highest pressure situations with fourth down and goal or third down and 15 yards in games when we were behind, and it's late in the fourth quarter," says Buchanico. He's cool as a cucumber when he's the one under pressure. But if it's one of his kids, Andy is a nervous wreck. He was red in the face and weak-kneed walking to the field that day. Then when Crosby started to sing, his face turned pale as a ghost's. Crosby belted that song out, and she was terrific, but he looked as if he might pass out until she finished. Afterward, he said to me, 'Darn, that's the toughest thing I ever had to do.' I said, 'I told you there was nothing to worry about. Now let's go play a football game.' He answered, 'Compared to what I just went through, the game will be a piece of cake.'"

Recently Mike Sherman asked his assistant, Susan Broberg to compile a list of the birthdays of the players' wives and children. Sherman personally signs each card. Yes, it's a small gesture but it lets everyone on the team know that he values family. Of course, he demonstrates that family comes first by the way he lives every day of his life. For instance, at the Packers' training camp, players are expected to stay in the nearby St. Norbert College dormitories, away from their families. But when Donald Driver's wife, Betina, was expecting a baby, Coach Sherman told his young player, "You need to be with your wife. You don't need to be in the dorm."

"But the rules are—" Driver started to say.

"I know what the rules are here," Sherman interrupted, "and they don't apply to soon-to-be fathers."

"She said it was up to me."

"It's okay, Donald. That's where you need to be."

All of our head coach clients are devoted husbands and fathers. And what better message on trust is there to send people than to demonstrate what kind of person you are? Simply put, these are good family men. My wife Lynn and I are proud to be associated with men of this caliber. We like doing business with good family people because, after all, we run a family business. By extension, we think of our clients as members of our family. Each of them is a close friend that we'd do backbends for, and we know they'd do the same for us.

A 2002 SURVEY TAKEN BY America's Research Group disclosed that 78 percent of the interviewees stated that they trusted a company that is active in the community. Eighty-one percent of the employees responded that the company's or the boss's giving increased their loyalty to their employer. The same survey maintained that giving also enhances a company's revenues because 63 percent of Americans stated they favored doing business with a company that is active in the community over one that is not. Sixty-two percent said they would purchase more goods and services from a company active in its community versus one that was not. These are cold facts that illustrate how employees and customers react to acts of charity.

Note too that the same ARG study revealed that a whopping 98 percent of Americans boasted that their bosses' civic activities made them feel proud about working for their employer. This is an amazingly high number. Imagine the impact it must have on boosting morale, which, in turn, enhances productivity. Knowing this emphasizes that it is not only good to give, it is good business! As we are told in the Parable of the Talents, what we give shall be returned to us tenfold. So while the purpose of corporate giving may not be to get something back in return, it does benefit the bottom line. Observe how the top Fortune 500 companies continue to make significant contributions to charitable organizations even during periods when the economy is weak. They do it because giving is built into their long-term budgets.

On other occasions, companies make business decisions to give generously internally. Providing your people with adequate health insurance coverage shows that you truly care for them.

A good leader instills trust in his people because he is consistently straightforward with them. He expects them to be the same with him. And he holds them accountable for what they say they will do. If a report is due at 10:00 on Wednesday morning, subordinates are expected to deliver it on time. Likewise, employees are expected to make sales, production, and budget figures. In a well-managed organization, people are held responsible for their performance. As John Fox says, "It's a production world that we live in."

When Mike Holmgren arrived in Green Bay, he made no attempt to emulate Vince Lombardi. Instead Holmgren chose to be his own man. This example should be followed by anyone in business who receives a promotion or is hired by another company to replace someone. For example, a popular manager might be promoted, transferred, or retire. No matter how esteemed he was by his subordinates, his replacement shouldn't try to copy him. When you try to be another person, at best you'll be a copy of him—a second-rate replica. Instead, be a first-rate original *you*. I've seen sons step in to replace their fathers whom they try to emulate—it rarely works. I've also observed CEOs of major companies try to emulate a popular predecessor. Again a big mistake! Likewise, when you replace somebody, be sure to say only good things about him. Never bad-mouth your predecessor.

A leader's strong work ethic sends a potent message that permeates an organization: The boss works hard and around here, hard work is rewarded. Successful business leaders lead by example. We've all seen bosses who arrive at the office in the late morning, take long lunch breaks, and spend excessive time on the golf course. "Do as I say, not as I do," they tell their people. This style of leadership undermines an organization because it makes people feel exploited. Strong leaders set a pace for others to follow. In most societies, a hard day's work is analogous to an honest day's pay. Translation: Hardworking managers are considered reliable and trustworthy. When Gruden came to Tampa Bay, his hard work ethic helped him win the trust of the organization.

Mike Sherman's confrontation with Warren Sapp demonstrated his genuine concern for his people. Similarly, a good business leader stands up for his people. I remember being told by an IBM sales rep about how she had been verbally accosted by a customer. After she reported the incident to her sales manager, he immediately confronted the customer. When the customer became hostile, the sales manager appropriately said, "IBM sales reps are trained to treat customers with courtesy and we expect customers to extend the same courtesy. I will not tolerate your ill behavior and I insist on an apology." Ultimately, the customer apologized. In another incident, I witnessed a burly customer shout obscene language at a mild-mannered sales clerk in a department store. A nearby supervisor rushed to the scene and politely asked the rude customer to leave the store. The customer tried bullying and intimidating the supervisor. Unnerved, the supervisor called two security guards, who promptly ushered the customer out of the store. The supervisor told the customer that he was not permitted to come back to the store. Store employees and other customers who witnessed the scene actually applauded the store manager for his action.

Employees judge their employers by the way customers are treated. If you're not fair with customers, what are you telling your employees? What will employees think about an employer who makes no attempt to live up to customers' expectations? What do employees think about working for a company that overcharges unsuspecting customers, gives poor service, puts fine print in customers' contracts, fails to live up to their warranties, and so on? Not only is it a bad way to conduct business, it plays havoc on internal morale. Why should an employee trust an employer who engages in shoddy business practices? "If my employer bilks customers, he'll do the same to me," thinks the employee.

Never forget that your people are always looking at you, judging you by your behavior—on and off the job. They evaluate you by the kind of family person you are. Being a faithful, loving spouse and parent sends a positive signal that you are trustworthy. Likewise, being an unfaithful spouse sends a negative message. How can you trust a person who doesn't honor a marriage contract to honor a business contract?

Trust is also earned by small, seemingly insignificant acts that demonstrate you care about your employees as people rather than revenue-producing assets. Spending quality time with employees in a nonbusiness atmosphere is an excellent way to get to know somebody. As the five coaches do on occasion, these get-togethers can be a round of golf, a bowling party, a dinner party, and so on. If your budget can't afford a fancy restaurant, invite a subordinate and his spouse to a home-cooked meal or a barbeque in your backyard. In fact, even if you can afford it, having them in your home is more intimate than a night out on the town. Send them cards on their birthdays and anniversaries. Send them emails and handwritten notes thanking them when they do good work. Listen to their suggestions. Stop by *their* offices to chat with them on occasion. When they're in your office, ask your secretary to hold calls. In short, make them feel important—because they are important. The sum of many small acts will be that people will know you care about them, and in turn, they'll respond by caring about you. The bottom line is caring employees are more productive.

4

Communication: A Two-Way Street

"Nature has given us two ears, two eyes, and but one tongue—to the end, we should hear and see more than we speak."

—SOCRATES (469–399 B.C.)

When making a speech, experience taught me to do my homework—knowing my subject is obvious. What's easy to overlook is the importance of knowing your audience. Keep in mind that what you say and how you say it will differ according to whom you say it.

For example, you'd speak differently to a group of teenagers than to an audience of senior citizens, even on the same subject. And a pep talk in a locker room wouldn't be the same as an inspirational speech in a church sanctuary. You must "read" your audience. No two audiences are the same, any more than two people are identical.

The kind of audience you are addressing determines everything from the content of the message to your delivery.

With a mother who was a dedicated schoolteacher, Jon Gruden was exposed to effective speaking at an early age. "I learned a great deal from the way my mom communicated with her students," he says. "She knew that every child in the classroom does not learn at the same level. Children's ability to comprehend varies according to their development, their family backgrounds, and a whole lot of other circumstances. To get through to all her students, she had to recognize their differences and teach by catering to their individual needs. The way she did this was by putting aside quality one-on-one time with each child. How else could she know what motivated a student to learn? I try to do the same thing. I want to know each of my players as an individual. Nobody wants to be known as just some generic guy.

"In any field, you constantly deal with people from different walks of life, different family backgrounds, different cultures. As a head coach, my job is to make sure every man is on board and ready to play at his best on Sunday. People respond to different motivations, and I've got to be able to understand what those are with each player. I have to push the right buttons."

"Jon doesn't want to put a player in a position where he might not excel with a given play," says Mark Arteaga, the head coach's assistant in charge of football operations. "He'll put a certain running back in for a play. He'll put a certain fullback in, a certain tight end, a certain receiver to run a particular route. Jon will make them feel, 'This play is just for me. The coach is working for me. He's trying to help me.'

"Jon tells them all the time, 'I want you to make millions of dollars. I want you to be good at what you do. I want you to be the best. Helping you do that is my job as head coach.'

"During the first few practices under Gruden, the players and coaches shook their heads, laughing to themselves because he was so intense. When they first saw him in action on the practice field, they were in shock when he called players out when they did something he didn't like. He got on them. He kept correcting them. But when they did it right, he loved them and he put his arms around them.

"When somebody didn't do it right, he let them know and everyone on the field could hear it. He showed no bias. 'What in the hell are you doing?' he'd shout. 'That's not what we went over in the meeting. Back on the ball and do it again.' Then they'd run the play again. 'Now that's what we're talking about. That's what we're looking for.' He got on them when they did it wrong and he explained the right way. And again he put his arms around them for doing it right.

"When a player saw Jon's passion and intensity, he knew the coach was trying to make him better, and if the individual gets better, the unit gets better, and the team gets better. Everyone understood that, and nobody resented Jon for getting on his case. The coach will call you out. He will expose you. However, he's not doing it to ridicule, criticize, or embarrass you. He just wants to take your game to the next level. Consequently, he's always in the back of your mind, and you're thinking, 'How would Jon want me to get this done? How should I do it?'"

Garrett Giemont, considered one of the NFL's top strength and conditioning coaches, joined the Buccaneers in 2003 after an eight-year hitch with the Oakland Raiders. Having worked with Gruden for four years in Oakland, Giemont has high praise for what he believes makes Gruden special as a leader. "His passion and endless energy separate him from any head coach I've been around," Giemont says. "Combine that with high intelligence, and when Gruden speaks, he truly knows what he's talking about. Nobody, absolutely nobody, debates this about him. Now, with all his knowledge, he is also a sensational communicator. Not only does he have a gift for speaking—he was a communications major—but the bottom line is he captivates his audiences.

"I liken Gruden to San Francisco Giants Hall of Fame pitcher Juan Marichal, who had many deliveries in his arsenal," continues Giemont. "Born in the Dominican Republic, Marichal would say in a thick Latin accent, 'I throw fast ball. I throw curve ball. I throw slider, knuckle ball. I throw palm ball, I throw change-up. But I throw it from here, here, here, and here.' The guy had 60 different pitches. Jon does too. He has many deliveries that he uses like Marichal—to fit the occasion. Jon has a matter-of-fact delivery. He has a little humor behind his delivery. He's got a kick-'em-in-the-ass delivery. He's got all kinds of deliveries in his arsenal, depending on who he's talking to, and he fits it to the individual.

"This is where God touched Jon on the forehead and gave him a gift. He gave him a presence so when he walks in a room, everyone knows it," Giemont explains. "As we say in this business, you can't coach that. You either got it or you don't got it! And that's what sets Jon Gruden apart from so many other coaches and from a hell of a lot of other people."

Giemont points out that Gruden excels at reading people, a faculty that allows him to communicate differently with each player, depending on the circumstance. "For instance, he talks differently to a star player than he does to a rookie," Giemont explains. "He'll do it out of respect to an individual who plays the game at a high level, someone with a strong work ethic who brings passion and knowledge to the table, day in and day out. At the same time, if somebody needs to be chewed out—if he has it coming—Jon isn't shy about reading the riot act to him. But he has a way of doing it so he doesn't offend the guy. That's because the guy knows he deserves it, and Jon is doing it for him and for the welfare of the team. The players have such respect for him that they don't resent it—and me personally, I love it. And anyone else worth his salt should love it too."

Being able to read people, Gruden is one of those people who always seem to say the right thing at the right time. He has savoir-faire. Something that would offend if said by someone else, Gruden can get away with. This, I believe, is a special knack that certain people develop over time. It's the result of exposure—a lot of it. Yet some people never get the hang of it.

Mike Sherman also excels at reading people. It's likely he developed this skill during his days as a teacher. He understands the importance of communicating with people at different levels because everyone is different. "The key is knowing how to reach each individual," Sherman explains. "Being an educator, I realize some guys learn better one way than another. For example, one player might do better by watching film. Someone else might see it better when it's physically demonstrated to him. This guy requires one-on-one instruction. Another learns better when taught in a group. And there is somebody else who needs to see it on paper. There are many ways to communicate with people, so you have to figure out what works best with each person. Consider too that while some people respond well to humor, some guys don't even have a sense of humor."

The people around Coach Sherman repeatedly say that one of his best attributes is his ability to sit down one-on-one with people. "He's a very good listener," says Susan Broberg, his administrative assistant. "The coach works hard to get to know his players, coaches, staff people, everyone. When you sit down with him, he makes you feel what you have to say is important and he respects your point of view. I've seen players go into his office with animosity, and when they leave, they're beaming. When I ask the coach what caused the big turnabout, he says, 'You know, Susan, when you get to know someone as a person, and you're honest with him, that usually will solve 90 percent of the problems.' In my opinion, Coach Sherman is the best at reading people I've ever known."

Vince Lombardi was bull-necked, gap-toothed, and had a voice that roared. Plus he had an explosive temper. Like the Green Bay coaching legend, Andy Reid looks every bit the part. Looks, however, are deceiving. Reid may look like he doesn't care one iota for you, but he does. Very much. So much, in fact, everyone around him knows that Reid truly cares about them. They see it in his eyes. He has a softness in his voice that lets them know he cares. This is what makes him a superb communicator—his sincere interest in people.

"Andy Reid is a master at figuring out what your psyche is," says head trainer Rick Burkholder, one of the most respected in his profession. "I've never seen anyone work at it to the extent he does. I was an assistant athletic trainer with the Steelers for six years, and I came here just a few weeks after Andy in '99. As the team's head trainer, one of my tasks is doing rehab work with injured players. Working for long stretches at a time with players, I get to know them very well and from a different perspective than the coaches. I also get feedback about players from the team's 24 part-time physicians, who report to me. Andy constantly seeks my input to learn more about this or that player, always wanting to know what makes him tick.

" 'What do you think about so-and-so?' Andy will ask me. 'Do I have to stand on his head? What do you think?' I'll give him my opinion, and then he'll ask the same question of a sports psychologist who works with the players. Then he'll ask the position coach, and one or two of my assistants. He keeps gathering information on people until he feels he fully understands them. Only then does he do anything. He's not an overreactive guy. He takes his time before he finalizes his thoughts.

"The other day we had a sports psychiatrist here, and Andy said to me, 'Get this guy with so-and-so, a new player.'

" 'Why? What's wrong with him?' I asked.

" 'Nothing.'

" 'Then why do you want the psychiatrist talking to him?'

" 'Because I don't know him. I want to know him. I want to know what he's about.'

"Now very few coaches that I have ever met will go to this length to know their players," Burkholder adds. "Some coaches have an informer in the organization who keeps them abreast of what the players are thinking. Andy doesn't need an informer because he constantly uses everyone in the organization to find out everything about everybody. His motive is pure. He wants to get everyone going in the right direction. If anyone has a beef, he wants to sit down with that person so he can nip it in the bud."

When it comes to knowing what's going on within the Eagles organization, Andy Reid is on top of everything. You might think of him as a "control freak," but Reid describes himself as a "mother hen." In addition to getting feedback from his coaches, he has several veteran players who act as informal coaches, and they too keep him aware of what the players are jawing about in the locker room.

To enhance communication, one of the first things Andy Reid did when he came to Philadelphia was to remodel the team meeting room in the basement of the old Veterans Stadium. Previously it was an L-shaped room, and when a speaker addressed the team, the defensive players and offensive players sat on opposite sides. Consequently, only the speaker could see both sides of the L by turning his head toward one or the other. When Reid eliminated that division, he had the room spruced up: fresh paint here, carpeting there, a green stripe down the walls, and so on. "With the wall removed, I

could see everyone's reaction at the same time when I stood in front
of my audience. Somebody should have knocked out that wall a long
time ago."

GREAT LEADERS CONSTANTLY COMMUNICATE WITH their people. In Tom
Peters' *In Search of Excellence,* a record-breaking bestseller business
book in the 1980s, Peters called it Management by Walking Around
(MBWA). He challenged business leaders to come down from their
ivory towers and spend time with assembly line workers in the facto-
ries, meet with office workers at their workstations, and call on customers in the field. Get to know them individually. *Listen* to what
they have to say. I agree with Peters. A majority of problems can be
solved simply by going to your internal people and listening to what
they tell you. Millions of dollars in fees from outside consultants can
be saved. That's because most solutions are out there with your people. But you have to go to them and hear them out.

Don't wait for people to come to you with problems. Be proactive. When there's a problem, strong leaders anticipate it. Whereas
most people are reactive and wait for a problem before they react,
strong leaders act beforehand, thereby preventing the problem from
happening!

"When I was being interviewed for head coach," John Fox says,
"management told me they were looking for someone with top communication skills. Well, some things don't come natural to me and I
have to work on them. But one of my strengths is my ability to communicate with people. It comes naturally to me. I spend a lot of time
with the players. I'm not a head coach that sits up here in his office
and gives orders to people. You won't find me here very often. I'm a

hands-on guy with my people. Look for me in the locker room, the weight room, or the ticket office. I'm constantly out there communicating with our people. At summer camp, I have breakfast early in the morning with the team. I don't sit at the coaches' table. I sit at a different table every day, and by the end of camp, I've had meals with everyone on the team. I constantly talk to my players. I go out of my way to stop someone walking by so I can talk to him. I say things to push their buttons. Because this is what's going to determine success or failure."

Jon Gruden understands the importance of getting down in the trenches with his people. During practice sessions, he instructs his team not only from the sidelines, he's out there on the playing field with the players. When Gruden first arrived in Tampa, the Bucs had already established themselves as one of the NFL's best defense teams. The team's offense, however, was lagging. So during his first week at training camp, in scrimmages, Gruden coached the offensive players by getting in their huddle with them. Going up against such All-Pro players as defensive tackle Warren Sapp and defensive safety John Lynch, Gruden might not appear as smart as he was billed. It's not that he chooses to be on the losing side. It's just that his mission—to get the offense up to par with the defense—is no small feat. So there Gruden was—in the middle of the offensive team's huddle, screaming and shouting, working in overdrive to fire up the players. "Okay, guys, let's keep ripping their asses," he shouts.

Later in the film room with the defensive unit, he told them, "I'm watching film on how to isolate number 47 (Lynch) in this first mini-camp, and I tell you, the first time you come on that weakside free-safety blitz, I'm going to buzz a slant right by your f——ing head. You won't know what hit you!"

★ ★ ★

MIKE HOLMGREN GETS FEEDBACK FROM a players' committee he set up to assure open communications. "Six players serve on it," he explains. "I personally pick them and I try to have an equal number of defensive players and offensive players, if I can. They're not the same players every year. The committee lets me know what the players are thinking. Sometimes a player has a beef I consider more fluff than substance. But through the committee, I find out if it truly is a big deal and this allows me to address it differently. Of course, everyone in the organization knows my door is always open. However, not all players feel comfortable coming to my office. They'd rather talk to the committee or a committee member, somebody who's a peer."

Because the nation's most notable leaders were exceptional orators, getting an audience fired up is often associated with great leadership. Since Abraham Lincoln delivered the Gettysburg Address, America's most memorable speech, millions of schoolchildren have put it to memory. Franklin D. Roosevelt inspired the nation in 1931 with his immortal words, "The only thing we have to fear is fear itself."

On May 5, 1961, John Kennedy challenged the nation to achieve what was long considered an impossible dream. The young president said, "I believe this nation should commit itself to achieving the goal, before this decade is out, of landing a man on the moon and returning him safely to the Earth." Kennedy boldly added, "No single space project in this period will be more impressive to mankind, or more important for the long-range exploration of space; and none will be so difficult or expensive to accomplish."

Martin Luther King Jr.'s 1963 speech, "I Have a Dream," became the battle cry for the civil rights movement in this country. Eloquence of great leaders can indeed alter the course of civilization. Business leaders with exceptional speaking skills can also fire up their people to tackle difficult challenges. Often, the presentation of a plan is what inspires a workforce to buy into it. I'd rather have a mediocre plan that people are excited about than a great plan that isn't supported. Remember, it's not only what you say it, but *how* you say it.

Jon Gruden recognizes the value of a spectacular presentation. He explains: "We have a prepared game plan for each Sunday, and it would be easy to just pass it out. But that wouldn't work. I've got to present our plays on the board during the week, and I've got to make those plays come to life. To do it right, I can't get up there and drift through the installation of a game plan. I have to work at it all Monday night and all Tuesday night, and when they come in here on Wednesday morning, I've got to dazzle them. I want them to be excited about the upcoming performance.

" 'This is the greatest play in this plan!' I tell them. And then when I get to the next picture, I tell them, 'This one is even better! If this play is called, it will score!' I say with enthusiasm and conviction. I'll show them a film that presents vivid examples of why it is going to work, and why it will be great. Hopefully, I build their confidence and they'll feel the same way I do. I've got to sell it to them, so when they go out to practice it, they believe in it, and they know when we call this play, we are together with it.

"We're no different than these fishing captains down here in Florida. You get the bait, you study the fish, you take your crew out there where you know the fish are biting, and you say, 'Let's go get them! Let's catch a bunch of them!' It's all about the presentation."

★　★　★

MUSIC IS ANOTHER OF THE tools Gruden uses to communicate with his players. He's been known to put on a player's headset to hear the music the player listens to. Sometimes, he'll use a lyric from a song to connect with a player. What do players think when they hear their head coach talking about Dr. Dre, Bon Jovi, Earth, Wind and Fire, or Prince? It means a lot to them. They've never been around a head coach who knows their music. Most important, Gruden understands their culture. He's in tune with their music and their movies and he can relate to them like no other great coach ever did. That lets players know that Gruden cares about them enough to learn their interests. As hectic as his work schedule is, he listens to their music.

Young players on the team love it when Gruden raps with them. I'd be surprised if any other head coach in the NFL can match him in this area. Evidently he finds time to watch MTV, although nobody is quite sure how he manages to do it. He'll even dub in a Biggie and Tupac song into game films. What does this do? It sends a message: "Hey, I'm one of you guys, and while I might be your head coach, I could get down with the best of you."

Gruden grew up with AC/DC. That's his rock group. He is still young enough to think back to his youth and recognize what young people want. He understands their love for music, and out of respect to them, he takes the time to learn it. Then, he'll hit them with a few lines he picked up in a movie, or a recording, and they look at him in amazement. It puts him on their wavelength. Or, as they say on the street, "You've got to feel the pulse." It's no different when the senior manager of a big company wants to relate to his workers on the assembly line. He has to approach them at a level where they feel comfortable. He can't dress in a $2,000 suit, be driven to the plant in a chauffeured limousine, and walk the line with an entourage of pin-striped executives and expect workers to feel comfortable with him.

Or to open up to him. There is no way this manager will feel the pulse of his people. He's not on the same wavelength.

To relate to people, you should discuss subjects that interest them. Do this and you'll get their attention. One of the Eagles' assistant coaches overheard a telephone conversation Andy Reid was having with his teenage daughter. "What do you think about Britney Spears and Justin Timberlake? I hear they broke up today." Knowing that Reid works long hours, the assistant was impressed. So was I. I'd be surprised if Reid ever heard Spears's or Timberlake's music. But that's not the point. He took the time to know something of interest to his daughter. That impressed me.

OUTSTANDING SPEAKERS ARE GOOD STORYTELLERS. I used the same technique when I taught history. I constantly wove anecdotal material into my lectures to make them come alive. Two teachers can teach the same history course—one will put his students to sleep, the other will stimulate them. Good nonfiction writers must do the same thing or their writing reads like a textbook. President Ronald Reagan, known as the Great Communicator, was a master storyteller. Professional speakers who are paid tens of thousands of dollars for a speech also use this technique. They do it to hold their audiences' attention, to entertain them. As a history teacher, I worked hard to make my classes entertaining. I used analogies to make history fun to learn. It's inexcusable for an educator to bore students! I constantly told my students, "History is an everyday event. Live it. Learn it. Enjoy it."

Jon Gruden is one of the all-time best storytellers. Plus, his stories are hilarious. Some of his stories make the players and coaches laugh so hard, they have to hold their sides. "An amusing made-up

story is often a way to get a point across, so I constantly speak with
analogies." Gruden explains. "For instance, a player was late for an
appointment with our head athletic trainer, Todd Toriscelli. Todd
stands five feet, six inches, and while he's actually from Steubenville,
Ohio, I told them an outlandish story about how he and I were buddies as kids. 'You may not know this. I grew up with Todd, and our
mothers, who were from Kentucky, took us there where we spent
our summers. His mom would make us delicious ham sandwiches.
Man, they were good! Now I don't want to get sidetracked so let me
tell you a quick story about Todd. I was 11, and Todd was 13, at the
time when we were playing on opposite Little League teams. Well,
he comes to bat and I'm the pitcher. I was one helluva Little League
pitcher. Man, I was dominant. I was the Sandy Koufax of the entire
league. Players were petrified to get into the batter's box when I was
on the mound. I was awesome. When I pitched, large crowds came
to the game. People talked about how I'd someday be in the majors.
It was just a matter of time. Let's get back to Todd now. He was only
this big and he steps to the plate. He's shaking. I whiz the ball right by
him and I strike him out. He never even got the bat off his shoulders.
Or to amuse myself, I'd bean him. Boy, did he get mad! Made him cry.
All summer. I'd either strike him out or get him with my beanball.

" 'Now Todd's grown up and he's your full-time trainer. Some of
you dorks are coming late for treatment. So what does Todd do? He's
throwing pills at me, and I don't like it. So get your ass in here and be
on time 'cause I'm tired of having Todd take out his anger on me.' I
was on a roll, and I kept going on and on, talking about Todd and me
growing up together. Of course, everyone knew it was all fabricated,
but they are loving it. And do you know what? I got my message
across. After that outlandish story, the players stopped being late for
their appointments with Todd."

Mike Sherman also likes to mix business with humor. This is evidenced by what Sherman does during a time that is otherwise serious business: game films reviews by players and coaches. Emulating his former boss, Mike Holmgren, Sherman has taken "film editing" to another level. For example, one night during a recent meeting at summer camp, everyone had assembled to watch a film. Standing at the head of the class with his back toward the screen, Sherman somberly announced, "It's been brought to my attention that some of you don't fully grasp the importance of the team meetings conducted during camp. It appears that certain individuals are of the opinion that the only thing that matters is what happens in the weight room and on the practice field. So to emphasize the importance of attending these meetings, we have prepared a film to show you that there is a right way and a wrong way to conduct yourself. The right way is to sit up, pay attention, take notes, ask questions, and so on. All of this will be demonstrated in this film we will show you. You will also learn the wrong way from some bad examples that appear in this film."

When the camera rolled, two of the younger players appeared on the screen. Rod Walker, a 320-pound defensive tackle, served as the good example. Wide receiver Robert Ferguson served as a bad example. Walker wore a three-button suit, tie, and bifocal glasses. In the film, Walker entered the room and immediately turned off his cell phone, sat up straight in his chair, and took out a notebook to take notes. He raised his hand and politely asked questions of the coach in the film. Then the camera focused on Ferguson. He was wearing a headphone and listening to rap music. A bottle of Jack Daniel's was sticking out his back pocket. He sat slouched in his chair, and his cell phone went off. He took brief naps, and inside his playbook was a hidden copy of *Playboy*. Throughout the film, the camera alternated between good example, bad example, good example, bad example. Roars of laughter began to fill the room.

Editing the film got even more creative when a scene from the 1999 movie *Life* was dubbed in. In *Life,* Eddie Murphy and Martin Lawrence play two small-time con men sentenced to life in prison for a murder they did not commit. In the movie, Murphy and Lawrence are seated at a long table in the prison's cafeteria, and Murphy wants to let the other prisoners know how tough he and Lawrence are.

Talking real bad, he says in a loud voice so all the prisoners can hear him, "We went on a minor killing streak all around the country. Killing people. All month, man. You all read about it in the papers. Sometimes you got to do certain shit. Just enough to let people know that you go where you need to go, to get it done. You push my button, there's no telling what I may do. Stab you. Choke you. Bite you. . . . You press the wrong button . . ."

Then, in the same scene, the camera had a close-up shot of a huge, 350-plus-pound prisoner (who bears a strong resemblance to Rod Walker) who shouts to the Lawrence character, "You gonna eat your cornbread?"

"You talking to me?" Lawrence asks.

"Yeah, he's talking to you," Murphy says.

"No, not at all. I want you to have it. Would you mind passing this down to—"

"No," Murphy says, "don't pass your cornbread to him. . . . That's your cornbread."

"Hey, I'm a grown man," Lawrence says. "Okay, I'm not gonna eat this cornbread. If he wants the cornbread, he can have it."

"If he wants the cornbread, let him go up to the front and get his own portion of cornbread. That's your cornbread. Hey, man, he's gonna eat his cornbread."

"I don't need you to take up for me. I'm all right. I'm a grown man. I can handle this," Lawrence says. "I'll give him my cornbread."

"If you let him have your cornbread," Murphy says, "you're going to be ironing his drawers and clipping his toenails."

"I ain't gonna be ironing—"

"Maybe I ought to eat your cornbread," the big prisoner says to Murphy.

Throughout the film, the camera cuts back and forth to the Robert Walker look-alike and the real Robert Walker. There would be Walker dressed in his pin-striped suit, talking earnestly about etiquette, and then his look-alike wearing prison garb. Each time the prisoner's image came in view, the players split a gut laughing hysterically. Ever since, it's an insider Packers joke that when somebody starts talking tough, another player will say, "Hey man, stop your cornbreading."

After Tampa Bay won Super Bowl XXXVII, football experts were predicting that the team was destined to become a dynasty under Jon Gruden. It didn't turn out that way. The Buccaneers struggled throughout the 2003 season. Going into the final stretch of the season with a 5-7 record and playing away at New Orleans, Gruden delivered an impassioned speech to his players the night before the game. "I saw the movie *Elf* with my boys," he said very seriously, "and I found out that Santa's sleigh runs on spirit. It doesn't run on gas and it doesn't run on just deer. It runs on spirit." Although he did his best to keep a straight face, he burst out laughing. So did the players. His humor had a calming feeling. On Sunday, the Buccaneers beat the Saints 14-7. In the world of business, humor can be an excellent antidote to ease tension. I think humor works particularly well in formal settings to break the ice whereas too much pomp and circumstance puts people on edge. So come down off your high horse and stop taking yourself or your business so seriously.

When Gruden is onstage, he tells hilarious stories and throws out rapid one-liners with such velocity, his audiences are spellbound. Indeed, he is one of the most entertaining persons I have ever met. In fact, each of the four other coaches also has a good sense of humor, and like Gruden, each uses it intermittently to relieve stress and to prevent monotony. Andy Reid can be whimsical; however, it's unlikely you'll see anyone bust a gut during an Eagles team meeting. Also a gifted storyteller, he's more witty, kind of folksy. A vintage Andy Reid line epitomizes his dry humor. It's a one-liner that came at the end of a team meeting on Saturday night prior to the Eagles' traditional dinner the night before a Sunday game. The meals are served buffet style and there's plenty of good food—steaks, hams, chicken, roast beef, hamburgers, and cheeseburgers. Nobody ever goes away hungry—and some of those big linemen have tremendous appetites. On this particular night, at the end of his talk, Reid wrapped it up by saying, "That's it. Come on, guys, I'll buy you a cheeseburger."

The players liked his cheeseburger line so much, it's become Reid's signature line, and inevitably at the end of a team talk, he says, "I'll treat you to a cheeseburger." And if he doesn't say it, the players are disappointed and somebody will say, "Hey, Coach, aren't you going to treat us to a cheeseburger?"

"Right. Come on, guys, I'll buy you a cheeseburger." A humble man, Reid is able to laugh at himself, an endearing trait that adds to his charm. Fans in Philadelphia are notorious for taunting other teams, and when their beloved Eagles are struggling, the crowd is prone to turn its anger toward the team and, in particular, the head coach. Butch Buchanico, who heads the Eagles' security department, recalls a time when he was escorting his boss through a rambunctious crowd following a hard-fought game that the Eagles lost in the final minutes. Among a lot of cursing and booing, one fan shouted at Reid, but the coach couldn't clearly hear it.

"What did he say to me?" Reid asked Buchanico.

"Forget it. It was nothing," Buchanico answered in a quiet voice, reluctant to offend Reid.

Reid picked up on the tone in Buchanico's voice. "You heard it, didn't you? It was something about cheesesteak, wasn't it?"

"If you have to know, Coach, the man said, 'Hey Andy, it looks like you've been eating too many Philadelphia cheesesteaks.'"

"Hey, I've never heard that one before. I like it. It's a good one. I'll have to remember it," Reid chuckled. "You know, Butch, I've really got to do something about this gut," he said, patting his stomach.

Andy had every reason to blow a fuse after a tough loss that Sunday, but that's not his style. Instead, he laughed at what was meant to be an insulting remark. That's the kind of guy he is. His self-deprecating humor has won the hearts and respect of this entire organization.

Gruden will use an anecdote to motivate the team. "It gets boring to simply say, 'We've got to play good defense and we've got to play good offense. And, oh, yes, we've got to have good special teams. And remember, we can't fumble.' So after getting our butts kicked three times in a row by the Eagles in Philadelphia, I told a story about home run hitter Barry Bonds. 'When I was living in California, I went to a San Francisco Giants game. The first time he goes to the plate, Bonds gets struck out looking. Second time up, he sawed off a little pop-up to the catcher. The third time, he strikes out again. Fourth time up, it's the eighth inning. What do you think Barry Bonds does? You think he takes his cuts. You think he takes a swing at the ball? You're damn right he does! He knocked that ball into the ocean—530 feet. Take your cuts. Get the bat off your shoulder. Hit these people. It's possible. You have it in you.'

"Then another time," Gruden continues, "I talked about the time I saw Tiger Woods in a golf tournament. 'Man, he's got good-looking broads at every hole. They're all going after Tiger, trying to distract him. Then there are racist bigots everywhere, trying to bring him down. The competition is fierce. Tiger is under all kinds of pressure. You know what he does? He birdies every hole. Shoots a 64. All you see is his fist pumping. He's not distracted. He's a pro. A stud. He's a mentally tough guy. It's possible. You have it in you."

Gruden's messages are entertaining as well as informative. When you hear him, it takes less than a New York minute to know that on the subject of football Jon Gruden is a maven. His vast knowledge wins the respect of his audience. His delivery is captivating. When he speaks, all eyes are glued on him. Nobody is looking at their watch or has their eyes fixed on the floor. They don't dare because if they do, Gruden is all over them. He has eye contact with everyone in the room. "It's as if I'm the only one in the room when he's talking," one player tells, "because he's looking right at me. But then the other guys say, 'No, man, he's talking directly to me.'"

"If I see a passive expression on someone's face," Gruden says, "I'll say to him, 'Right, Bob?' or 'Got that, Bob?' To someone else, I'll say, 'Sam, you with me?' or 'Nice hat, Jack.' I do this to keep my audience on their toes and get them involved. You know, audience participation.

"After my speech, I'll say to a player, 'Say, what's the matter with you? Am I boring you? Let's fix it, man. Want me to tell you a bedtime story and put you to sleep tonight?' That usually gets a little laugh out of him. I do what I can to get them to see my point without creating animosity.

"Now don't get the idea that it's all fun and games," Gruden continues. "This is a business, and sure, we have a little fun. But I like to mix it up; otherwise, if it's only X's and O's, over the long season it does get monotonous. I like to keep it interesting."

John Fox uses humor to quell tense times. For instance, during a hard workout at the Panthers' summer training camp in Charlotte, the players were exhausted. The temperature was in the high 90s, the humidity was as thick as water, and there was not a cloud in the sky. The sun was red-hot. At a break on the field, Fox told them, "You know, guys, it just doesn't get any better than this. What you're getting here at training camp, people pay thousands of dollars to get at luxurious health spas. Look what you get here and it's free. We feed you, and man, I don't have to tell you how good the food is. What's more, all of your meals are prepared by nutritionists. You get to eat as much of it as you want. You have this wonderful exercise program. You've got physical therapists here. I'm telling you, it just doesn't get any better than this. Life is good, guys."

IT WAS LATE IN THE season at Lambeau Field in Green Bay, and the Packers were playing Pittsburgh on a subfreezing Sunday afternoon. With little time left on the clock, the Packers were trailing the Steelers. It was third and two, and Coach Holmgren called a time-out. He huddled with his young quarterback Brett Favre on the sidelines. Quarterbacks Mark Brunell and Ty Detmer joined in.

"We had 45 seconds to talk and make a decision," Holmgren explains. "I said to Favre, 'If we make this first down, we have a chance of winning this game. I'm looking at two plays I like. Which one do you like best, Brett?'

"I quickly reviewed the two plays, and he didn't say anything. He just had this goofy expression on his face. Finally, I banged him on the chest to get his attention, and I said, 'Hey, look at me.'

"'Mike,' he goes, 'you ought to see your mustache now.'

"I go, 'What?' I put my hand to my face, and icicles had formed on my mustache. I was wearing this big hat and I must have looked like Wally the Walrus.

"Brunell and Detmer split a gut laughing. Here we were in a crisis moment, and that's all they can do. It cracked me up too. Favre has a wonderful sense of humor, and as I look back, his timing for exhibiting humor was just perfect. It took the edge off the stress and we were able to think more clearly."

I've known Mike Holmgren for a quarter of a century, and no matter how stressful his job gets, he has never taken his work so seriously that he's devoid of humor. Mike is one of those people with a self-deprecating sense of humor. He doesn't mind making himself the butt of the joke.

The night before game day, the entire team watches game films. "Every now and then to keep everyone's attention," Holmgren says, "I'll have something dubbed into the film at the tail end that has nothing to do with football. It's something that pokes fun at one of the players, but more often than not, it pokes fun at me. For instance, I used to sing in a rock-and-roll group called Big Bop and the Choppers. One of our coaches had our film guy edit a part of an old film, and he put it into one of our highlight tapes. So suddenly, out of nowhere, there I am, singing a solo. I'm 'Manifold Mike King of the Grease Pack.' I'm singing some song with that '50s music that goes, 'Sha na na.' Our guys are cracking up. Some are literally falling off their chairs!"

As I earlier discussed, Mike Holmgren and I go back a long time and I can tell you he can be as tough as the most hard-nosed Marine drill sergeant at boot camp. Even the biggest, toughest 300-pound-plus defensive lineman cowers when Holmgren reads the riot act. Trust me, nobody wants to be on the receiving end of a Holmgren reprimand. And if you ever are, and you stand up to him, you damn well better be right. Otherwise, be prepared for all hell to break loose. For the most part, however, Holmgren is fun-loving and thrives on seeing people have a good time. For example, a few years ago on Halloween, when everyone had assembled for the team's ritual morning meeting, Holmgren walked in wearing a costume. For those who were there, seeing this six-five mountain of a man dressed in an elf costume was a sight to behold. Why does he carry on like this from time to time? "It breaks down communication barriers," he explains. "It lets people know I'm approachable.

"The players love this stuff. I like to do these kinds of things with the players because it gives them a break from the stress they're under during summer camp and the regular season. Considering that we have five preseason games, 16 season games, and as many as four playoff games, it's a long time that we do the same thing over and over with the same people. It gets very serious. During the season, Thursday is generally my day for humor because it helps to break up the week. The humor is mainly stupid stuff, but by Thursday, it doesn't take much to get a laugh around here."

"IN 2002, MY FIRST YEAR with the Panthers," says John Fox, "General Manager Marty Hurney asked me, 'How do you know you're getting through to the players?'

"We'll know it," I told him, "when we get to where we want to be, and the players are saying the same things I am saying. It's my opinion that leadership is getting people to do something, but it's also selling them on wanting to do it. And they believe it. That's when I'll know I'm getting through to them."

Andy Reid agrees. "I listen to what the players say during postgame interviews with the media. I hear a lot of things their coaches told them in the locker room. Lines like, 'Somebody has to step up and make the big play.' A player will say, 'Who's it going to be?' When I hear comments like that, it lets me know we are getting through to them. This to me is the real test."

It's interesting that none of the five head coaches in this book played in the NFL during his younger days. Hall of Famers Otto Graham and Norm Van Brocklin were among the best quarterbacks who ever played this game. Yet they weren't great coaches, because they were unable to relate to players that weren't as talented as they were during their playing days. To Graham and Van Brocklin, the game came instinctively. They were unable to communicate their know-how to players. Hence it didn't transfer.

THERE'S NO QUESTION THAT WHEN great leaders speak, people listen. Of course, not everyone is a "natural-born" speaker. However to be a business leader, you must develop some proficiency as a public speaker; your failure to do so will severely handicap your chances to succeed. I am cognizant that some people have limited speaking skills—they have a weak voice, a stutter, and so on. Having said this, there are professionals who can coach you to be a decent public speaker. If you're determined to lead others, you must put the time and effort into acquiring these skills. Remember now, leadership is not for everybody. Some people are more blessed with God-given talents that make them natural leaders. A majority of people will never lead others.

The quickest way for a speaker to bomb is to have a "canned" speech that doesn't take into account that every audience is different. As we say in football parlance, you must be able to cut on the run. In other words, you must be able to read your audience, and if you're losing it, you adapt by cutting from your prepared speech and move on to the next topic. This is difficult for a novice speaker. It's a skill that takes time to develop because it comes over time with experience. Meanwhile, the better prepared you come to speak, the more flexibility you'll have to switch gears. Being prepared is the key because it enhances your confidence. Notice how outstanding speakers radiate self-confidence.

We've all sat through enough speeches and sermons to realize that it borders on being criminal to deliver a boring speech. Like some of the coaches who have started to dub game films with humor, I recommend it to business leaders who give visual presentations. Some managers ask, "Is it appropriate to use humor during a very serious presentation?" Yes, and may I add, particularly so. A little humor goes a long way during a long, tedious financial presentation, especially to a group of marketing people with little finance background. The same is true when making a technical presentation to nontechnical people. Certainly common sense dictates use of humor in good taste.

I know of one such presentation recently given by a CEO who had images of five of his top executives, as well as himself, as young men back in the early 1970s—they all sported long sideburns and were dressed in leisure suits—and there they were, these comic images projected on a screen. The CEO, who is now bald, had shoulder-length hair! Self-deprecating humor of this nature sends a positive message to an organization. It's healthy for people to be able to laugh at themselves. It demonstrates that they are good guys who are approachable. No leader wants to isolate himself in an ivory tower, removed from his people.

All too often, business leaders deliver bland speeches that put their audiences to sleep. Adding a spice of humor goes a long way toward enlivening an otherwise dull speech. There's no reason why a business speech can't be entertaining *and* informative. A timely joke is not only a great icebreaker, relaxing an audience at the beginning of a speech; it keeps them alert—they listen carefully because they don't want to miss something funny! Then too, humor connotes wit and cleverness, both positive attributes of a successful person.

Public speaking is only one facet of needed communication skills required to effectively lead others. Great leaders excel at relating one-on-one with people. Here too, they do their homework and take the time to know their people. They are constantly asking questions, always seeking to find answers. I advocate that anyone in a managerial position should understand the psyche of his or her subordinates. This requires strong listening skills. Remember, God gave us two ears and one mouth, so we were meant to listen twice as much as we speak. Certainly, listening is an imperative communication skill, yet great leaders are commonly visualized in a speaker's role rather than a listener's role. Successful business leaders always have an antenna up so they can hear what their employees, customers, and competitors are saying.

Successful business leaders don't hide behind closed office doors; they walk the floor—they meet with their people who work in plants, warehouses, laboratories, and places in remote locations. They do this on a regular basis so they can know firsthand what their people are thinking. And they listen carefully to what people are saying, knowing their employees are the best sources of advice for solutions to company problems. Why? Because nobody better understands their jobs than a company's own employees—outside consultants included, and may I emphasize especially outside consultants. You will find that a vast majority of the solutions to your problems are within the walls of your organization. Your people have the solutions; listen to them and they will provide them!

Forget about eating in the executive dining room or going to your private club for lunch. Eat in the company's main cafeteria and, like John Fox does, take turns sitting with people at all levels of the organization. Try this or—if your company doesn't have a cafeteria— take subordinates out for lunch. It doesn't have to be a fancy restaurant. They'll appreciate your interest in them far more than an expensive meal. You'll be surprised what you can learn from your people once you make them feel comfortable in your presence. Be yourself with them. Don't feel like you always have to act as the boss. If you cease to be a real person, you cease to be a real leader.

And when you spend time with your subordinates, make a point of not limiting your conversations strictly to business. Get to know them. Find out about their families, their golf game, their hobbies, and their interests. Listen. Show them that you're sincerely interested in them as human beings, not just as salaried employees who make money for the company.

5

Teamwork: We Win Together

"Individual commitment to a group effort—that is what makes a team work, a company work, a society work, a civilization work."

—VINCE LOMBARDI

The Packers are to Green Bay what gambling is to Las Vegas, what fine dining is to New Orleans. If it were not for its NFL franchise, most Americans would have never heard of Green Bay, Wisconsin.

With a population of 102,726, Green Bay is America's smallest city with an NFL franchise. There is not a close second. Founded in 1919 by E. L. "Curly" Lambeau and George Whitney Calhoun, the Packers joined the American Professional Football Association three years later. At the time, Green Bay's population was less than 20,000! In 1925, City Stadium was constructed, a 32,000-seat facility. Following the death of the team's founder and first coach, the stadium was renamed Lambeau Field in 1965. The newly renovated Lambeau Field has a seating capacity of 72,515. Season tickets have been sold out every year since 1960. Lambeau Field is proof of the home team advantage. The Packers regular-season home game record since 1992 is 75-13, plus a 6-1 mark in the playoffs, an overall record of 81-14 (.852).

The Green Bay Packers, Inc., has been a publicly owned, non-profit organization since 1923. There are 4,748,910 shares outstanding that are owned by 111,507 shareholders. It is the only publicly traded professional sports team in America. With so many shareholders, it is truly a franchise owned by its fans. To keep anyone from having control, the articles of incorporation prohibit any shareholder from owning more than 200,000 shares. Annual shareholder meetings are held in an arena across the street from the Packers' headquarters; attendance exceeds 3,000.

Packers fever is so strong, it's doubtful if there's a single person in Green Bay who doesn't have a piece of green-and-gold clothing in his or her wardrobe. Upon being ushered into this world, newborns at local maternity wards are wrapped in green-and-gold blankets. How's that for developing brand identity with an eye on long-term market share!

Due to its size, Green Bay is unique among cities with professional teams. Sure, there are fanatics wherever sports are played. But nothing matches how the *entire* community gets behind the Packers in this Midwest community. Certainly, much of the fervor has to do with the fact that the Packers are the only game in town. Without its football franchise, Green Bay is just another Great Lakes port where the local citizenry packs and ships meat. It's unlikely that the local chamber of commerce could drum up much civic pride by presenting itself as a meatpacking center. The Packers, however, are entirely another story. The team puts Green Bay on the map. Big-time. Remember too that the Packers are no ordinary NFL team. In October 2002, a survey conducted by Harris Interactive named the Packers as America's favorite football team, replacing the Dallas Cowboys, which had held the title for nine consecutive years. In its February 3, 2003, issue, *ESPN, The Magazine* named the Packers as the best franchise among the 121 teams in the four major sports.

Green Bay's small-town charm creates an atmosphere that fosters a team spirit unlike any other franchise in professional sports. As Mike Sherman explains, "Even though this is an NFL franchise, I sometimes feel like I'm coaching at a small-town high school in Wisconsin, Ohio, or Texas. Everywhere I go, people say, 'Hey, Coach, what are we gonna do this week?' and 'You gotta beat the Vikings. They gave us trouble last time.' Everyone has an opinion, and they're going to be at the game. There's no escape. High school coaches in small towns can't escape it. Neither can I.

"Coaching here is unlike any other job in the League," Sherman continues. "My two boys, Matthew and Benjamin, are in school a half mile from my office, and my daughter Emily's high school is a mile from here. I live five minutes away. I can have lunch with my kids, go to their ball game, and be back here later in the day. Even my daughter Sarah who attends Marquette University in Milwaukee is only two hours away. On Saturday mornings, I have a team practice, and afterward I can stop to see my son play football in the park and still catch a plane in the early afternoon. The accessibility is fantastic. The players live only minutes from Lambeau Field, which also means we all live near each other. We have a tradition in which the players ride bicycles back and forth from the locker room to the practice field during summer camp. In other cities, players live 30 minutes or an hour away and are spread out in all directions. We're all neighbors here, and this makes us a very close-knit group. This proximity is wonderful for building a team atmosphere. There's nowhere else in national football where everyone lives so close together. We're like family here."

On a personal note, my daughter Lori is married to Dan Knopps from Rhinelander, Wisconsin, a town of 9,000 just 100 miles or so northwest of Green Bay. When the Knopps family found out I represented Mike Sherman, they enthusiastically accepted me into their family.

"The team has a tremendous impact on the community," tells Susan Broberg, Sherman's assistant. "People live and die with this team. When you live here, the Packers are a part of your everyday life. Although I've never seen the numbers, I'd bet that if an economic study were done, it would show that people here spend less money after a loss. People take it so much to heart when we lose, you see fewer people in restaurants, bars, and even shopping malls. I remember when we came back from New Orleans after winning the Super Bowl in '97. The city had a parade scheduled to start downtown and conclude with a celebration in the stadium, a route that was estimated to take 30 minutes. Team members were on buses and the windows were kept open so they could wave to the crowds. With the temperature at 10 below, we figured a half hour was ample time for a parade. The streets were so mobbed with people that the parade took more than three hours to complete. Everywhere you looked, there were camera bulbs flashing and people holding signs with messages expressing their appreciation for a great season. There was so much devotion and pride of ownership you could feel it in the air. Of course, many of the fans are owners, so they actually do own the team."

All this pride in the beloved Packers places an added responsibility on the team's leader, Mike Sherman, that no other NFL head coach has. It's an uplifting feeling to know the entire community is behind you. But during a losing season, the pressure is immense. As the Packers' head coach, Sherman is definitely a big fish in a small pond. All eyes are on him, more so than the mayor or the governor.

It's a two-way street. The Packers also support the community. The organization's mission statement reads:

> *The Green Bay Packers organization is committed to working to improve the lives of the people in all walks of life in Wisconsin and Upper Michigan. As highly visible members of the community, the Packers' players, coaches and staff acknowledge their unique public role and are devoted to working with charities, schools, civic groups and other outreach sources to make positive contributions throughout the area. The Packers welcome the opportunity to give back to the community that has steadfastly supported the team for more than 80 years.*

These are not idle words. Two full-time employees and one part-time employee spend every working day organizing charitable and civic involvement that ranges from appearances to donations. Many of the community activities focus on children, where as good role models, the players serve as a positive influence on the community's youth.

"There is a great sense of history and tradition in the Green Bay Packers," Sherman says. "When you coach here or put on our green-and-gold uniform, you think about the organization and what it represents. The fact that the ultimate prize in the National Football League is the Vince Lombardi Trophy serves as a reminder that the Packers are not measured by winning ball games, but by winning championships. A lot is expected of our team, and as the head coach, I make sure our players and coaches know it.

"A renovation program to upgrade Lambeau Field began in 2000, and upon its completion in 2003, stadium capacity increased from 60,890 to 72,515. During the construction, the contractor started tearing up the old tunnel underneath the stadium where the players exited onto the field. 'A lot of great teams went through that tunnel,' I told them, 'and it's part of our history.' I had the contractor take big chunks of concrete out of that tunnel and place them on the surface of our new tunnel. I wanted our players to walk over the same concrete to let them know they belong to the same team as those former Packers. There's also a plaque on the concrete to make sure everyone knows it. It also reminds them that they have a history behind them, and when they go through that corridor, they represent the Green Bay Packers. They carry a big tradition on their shoulders."

Sherman also saved the doorframe to Lombardi's office in the older building and it's now the entrance to his office. He did it to remind himself of the big shoes he has to fill. A copy of one of Lombardi's old playbooks is prominently displayed on his desk. Sherman enjoys flipping through it to remind him about how the game has since changed—and how much it hasn't. He also put up photographs on the walls between the locker room and the field that display highlights of the most memorable moments in Lambeau Field history. These include action photos of former Packer greats such as Don Hudson, Paul Hornung, Bart Starr, Jim Taylor, and Ray Nitschke.

As busy as NFL coaches are, I don't think many others would pay as much attention to old traditions as Sherman. I view it as good leadership. Sherman understands the value of instilling a strong sense of pride in his organization. A sense of pride inspires people. It makes them feel that the team is bigger than the individual.

Tampa is no Green Bay. Unlike the Packers, the Buccaneers don't have a monopoly on being the entire community's favorite pastime.

With a metropolitan area population of 3.6 million, it's no sleepy town in the Midwest where there's not much else going on. There is no shortage of recreation on Florida's west coast on the Gulf of Mexico. With one of the best climates in North America, year-round activities are abundant. There are beaches, golf, tennis, fishing, and boating. Tampa has a full menu of the performing arts, including legitimate theater, opera, symphony, and ballet plus museums and art galleries. Unlike Green Bay, Tampa is a major tourist destination. Certainly, the Bucs are a draw, but this NFL franchise is not the only game in town. And while there is plenty of civic pride, unlike the Packers, it's not exclusively focused on its professional football team. However, like the Packers, there is considerable pride within the Buccaneers organization. It was there when Tony Dungy was head coach and has been enhanced since the arrival of Jon Gruden.

I've visited most of the franchise headquarters in the NFL, and Tampa Bay's facility ranks at the bottom of the heap. It's been the home of the Buccaneers for 20-plus years, and most of the other franchises have since erected state-of-the-art buildings. For instance, the Eagles and the Packers moved into elaborate headquarters just before the start of the 2003 season. One Buccaneers Place can't hold a candle to these state-of-the-art facilities. Nonetheless, the players affectionately refer to Raymond James Stadium as "the woodshed." This moniker originated when Jon told the team, "We have the most beautiful facility in the NFL. What's so special about One Buccaneers Place is that we don't take the garbage out, we spit on the floors, we leave our towels everywhere—and we love it! It's our house. It's our woodshed."

Before home games, the players will say, "We're going to take them to the woodshed," in reference to giving the visiting team a beating.

"We don't have the greatest facility," Gruden admits. "Every day, we have every excuse to bitch about it. But if you look at it positively, you can say with pride, 'One Buccaneers Place is the best facility in football.' Why is it the best? Because it's ours. We've got the best players in the world. Why? Because they're ours. We're going to have a better practice than everybody else. Why? Because it's our practice. This is how we think around here. I've got to coach that. I can't just coach X's and O's."

To instill pride in his players, Gruden likes to show films of Tampa Bay games from the "old" days. "I'll take films that feature players like Vinny Testaverde throwing a long touchdown pass, or Lee Roy Selmon sacking the quarterback. Some of our players know who Selmon is but they never saw him play. 'Do you want to see the hardest sack you've ever seen?' I'll say to them. 'You want to see a helluva thrill? Watch this throw.' I show film of some of our greatest players to let them know that this is their heritage. I want them to be filled with pride when they go out on the field because they play for Tampa Bay where so much is expected of them."

Jon likes to use a line that I also use. "Invest in yourself," he frequently says to his players. "You've got to put the time into running, lifting, studying, going to meetings. You do it on and off the practice field. I expect you to make yourself a better person. Not only a better individual, a better teammate. Do it for yourself. Do it for the team."

IN CERTAIN ATHLETIC ENDEAVORS, AN athlete competes on his own. The grueling hours during which he prepares to compete are spent in solitary confinement. When a boxer steps into the ring, it's just him against his opponent who wants to knock his head off. The runner, the swimmer, the golfer, the singles tennis player, and the downhill skier—each faces victory or defeat, depending on his individual performance. In comparison with team sports, there are no teammates to depend on or to be held accountable. Nor is there camaraderie. Success is based on individual effort. There are no teammates to lift his spirits after a defeat. No teammates to rejoice with after a victory. Such is the life of the lone-wolf athlete.

In contrast, football is the ultimate team sport. Each of the 11 players on the field must execute his assignment during the course of a single play—the success or failure of the entire team depends on it. Andy Reid played as an offensive guard and tackle during his high school and college days. His modest, selfless nature as a head coach is attributed to his years spent as a lineman. "I'm glad to be of offensive lineman roots," he states. "Coming from this background you don't lose perspective amidst the glamour, the monetary things. You have that hard-work thing ingrained in your brain. You understand you haven't gotten to where you are without hard work."

With Reid's offensive lineman's mentality, the Eagles' head coach talks a lot about "mastering the box." The box he makes reference to is the three-by-three-foot space around a lineman that is the world of this player. "You've got a three-by-three-foot box," he tells his offensive linemen. "That's your territory. You line up for a play. That's where you go. The defensive lineman facing you is a much better athlete. He's faster and probably quicker and stronger than you. He's coming at you, so he has an advantage of knowing where he's going." Reid likes to remind a lineman that the reason he's playing on the offensive line is that's the only position he can play. It's probable that the offensive lineman doesn't have the athletic ability to play any other position. He was an offensive lineman in high school and college. And although he's going against a superior athlete, on most plays the offensive lineman wins the battle. He makes the blocks. He has one responsibility. Master the box.

The five offensive linemen work together, each one controlling his three-by-three foot turf. When they take control of the line, the chances of a successful run, pass, or kick are vastly improved. When every player executes his responsibilities, the team wins. The process anticipates variables, breaks them down, and neutralizes them. This is what teamwork is all about. Everybody executes his job. There are no exceptions. This is what winning teams do. It's a team effort—on the football field, in the workplace.

"Andy provides an excellent working environment," explains the Eagles' offensive coordinator Brad Childress. "It's very businesslike. Guys get here early, they stay late. They work hard during the day. It's no different than any other business. You spend time at your trade and you work hard at it. Like Jimmy Valvano, who won the NCAA basketball tournament in 1983 when he was head coach of North Carolina State, would say, 'Working hard gives you a chance to have a chance.' It's a given, if you don't work hard, you are going to get your tail kicked."

At the end of the 2001 season, a staff meeting was called that included everyone in the entire Eagles organization. Reid thanked every person in the room. "We all have a job to do. Everyone's job is important. It's marketing, it's public relations, it's football. It's everybody right on down to the receptionist and right on up. I want to thank each of you for your hard work. We didn't get as far as we would have liked to, but we couldn't have gotten this far without everybody. I appreciate what each of you contributed."

Butch Buchanico, who was in charge of game day operations in 2001, recalls the Eagles head coach congratulating him after a Philadelphia win. "Coach shook my hand and told me what a great job I did. Then he added, 'I want you to tell people that everybody is a part of this. I'm talking about the crew that cleans the stadium. The vendors who sell hot dogs. The plumbers. The mechanics. They're all on my team. When you talk to them, Butch, you can tell them that I said if they succeed, we are all going to succeed.' At my game day meetings, I'd address these people and tell them what Reid said. At first, they were taken aback—they weren't used to receiving kudos from the top."

Reid's assistant, Carol Wilson, remembers saying to Reid after a big win, "Congratulations. That was a great game."

"Congratulations to you too, Carol," he replied.

"He makes everyone feel that he or she had an important role in the win," she explains. "When we win a big game, Coach gives a game ball to someone. I nearly fainted when he announced after one game, 'This game ball is presented to Carol Wilson.' He sure knows how to make us all feel like we're part of the win. I actually have two game balls. I have them displayed. Those two game balls are something nobody else will have."

Andy Reid has such a steady temperament that when the Eagles lose, he maintains such an even disposition that without knowing the final score of a game, an observer wouldn't know which team won. Certainly, he takes every loss personally. After an Eagles loss, he keeps himself in his office and reviews game films—the same ones, again and again. As Wilson explains, "I can tell when he's upset, so I'll try to console him by saying something like, 'That was a tough one to lose,' and he'll just say, 'Yeah, yeah, yeah.' Then he just stays to himself until he gets it all together in his own mind. Later, he'll come out of his office and might say something like, 'We didn't do this,' or 'We should have done that,' and then it's, 'Let's get on with it.'

"As we get into the season, he usually gives the players Monday and Tuesday off," Wilson continues. "Unlike some coaches, if the team loses a big game, Andy doesn't punish them by making them come in on Monday for practice. In his mind, we are a team to win, and we are a team to lose. He won't blame it on one person. He doesn't say, 'He missed this,' or 'He should have done that.' If he does have a problem with a player, he lets him know, but it's in private. The players respect him for this. Some coaches blame a loss on a particular player when they talk to the media. They'll do it indirectly to get their point across. That's not Andy's style. He's too classy to do that."

As an ex–offensive lineman in high school and later at Brigham Young University from 1979 to 1982, Reid spent the next nine years primarily as a college offensive line coach before landing an NFL job with the Packers in 1992. At Green Bay, he was a tight ends and assistant offensive line coach for four years, and then spent the next two years as a quarterback coach. In this capacity, he worked with Brett Favre, who under Reid's guidance was named the League's Most Valuable Player in 1997 and 1998. Reid gives credit to Holmgren for advising him to learn the entire offensive system inside and out, not just the offensive line and tight ends positions. "He'd always be asking questions about everything," Holmgren recalls, "always taking notes, jotting everything down. He was like a sponge, wanting to learn as much as he could."

Andy Reid may have an offensive lineman's mentality, but he clearly understands that the five players on the offensive line represent a single crucial piece of a complex puzzle; still, all pieces must fit perfectly to complete the puzzle. As Philadelphia's head coach, Reid has proven he knows where the pieces go. This is where he epitomizes teamwork, which is getting everyone to work together in harmony— meaning the combined sum is greater than individual efforts. Reid demonstrated how this works near the end of the 2002 season. Pro Bowl quarterback Donovan McNabb and backup Koy Detmer were both on the disabled list for the Eagles' last five games of the regular season. "McNabb is one of the great stars in the National Football League," Reid explains, "and when your field general is down, you have to call on your next guy to step up. Koy stepped in for Donovan but then he suffered an elbow injury so we brought in A. J. Feeley to start at quarterback, his first NFL start. This was his second year in the NFL and he had thrown only 13 passes for Oregon during his senior year. A. J. stepped up to the plate, leading us to win four out of our last five games and we went to the playoffs. McNabb recovered and guided us to a 20-6 victory over Atlanta. The following week we got beat by Tampa Bay, the team that ultimately won the Super Bowl."

"Under Andy's leadership, everyone in our organization believes in the system," explains Childress. "We can plug people into our system—it's all the parts and the whole. Each player must understand what his job entails." Andy doesn't want them thinking about winning or losing games. He'd rather have them focused on doing their assignment. When everyone does, the team succeeds. That's why we were able to bring in Koy when Donovan was injured, and repeat the same process when A. J. came in to replace Koy. Sure, the media may make it seem like this is a one-man team with Donovan McNabb and a cast of thousands. But the fact is, we are a team. Our guys are professional. They're prideful."

JOHN FOX PLAYED DEFENSIVE BACK in high school and college, and after graduating in 1977 he spent most of his career as a defensive backs coach. In 1994, he became defensive coordinator for the Oakland

Raiders and later worked four years (1997–2001) with the same title building the New York Giants' great defensive unit. Unlike a lineman or linebacker, a defensive back has a full view of coverages, and in this capacity he can see the whole picture. This is where John Fox comes from—ever since he played football in high school, he has observed how each player contributes to the success of the entire team.

"Unlike many head coaches," explains defensive lineman coach Sal Sunseri, "Foxy teaches his players the concept behind the play. This enables players to understand what their teammates are responsible for. John's philosophy is that if you know what the guy next to you does, you'll more clearly understand what you're supposed to do. When everyone on the team understands, players can feed off each other. John believes that if they understand the concept of the play rather than just their own role, they'll perform better. This is a different approach than the coach who says, 'The only thing you need to know is your assignment.'"

"Starting from infancy, we all go through life depending on people," says Fox. "I am dependent on my mother, my father, my brothers. We are always dependent on other people. Girlfriends, wives. Teamwork is the same way. We depend on each other, and we have to be there for each other.

"I spend a lot of time with group dynamics, talking to my players about having respect for each other," Fox continues. "As head coach, my job is to deal with the interrelationship of groups of people that come from diverse backgrounds. I've got to continually sell them on teamwork. *'It's not just about me!'* I keep repeating. For instance, I had a couple of guys that dressed in a new style on a road trip. While they didn't actually break a dress code, I explained to them, 'I appreciate your individuality, but we are a team. And when you're a member of a team, you don't always get to do exactly what you want to do.' I went on to tell them that in life, you have to invest—you can't just spend. 'Whether you're investing in a relationship with a teammate, a coach, your wife, or your kids, you've got to invest in it, not just spend it.' As you can see, a head coach has many roles. He's a sports psychologist, a father, a big brother, a teacher. . . .

"This is a team sport and to win, the players have to place the team above themselves," Fox adds. "In a close game, for example, with little time remaining, a back or a receiver might have to step out-of-bounds to stop the clock even though he could have picked up a few more yards by staying in-bounds. Sure, those extra yards might enhance his personal statistics, but in this situation, it hurts the team. The seconds he saves are more important to the team than the yards he gains.

"It's a given that a player wants what's best for him and his family. At the end of the day, everyone does. At the same time, everyone has to realize that what's best for the team is also best for him. We succeed or fail as a team. When we lose a game, I don't say to them, 'We got outplayed.' I say, 'We got outplayed, outcoached, out-everything.' When you start building trust in a team, it's not management versus the players or vice versa. You never want to create an atmosphere that fosters 'It's me against management' or 'It's me against the League.' Everyone has to think, 'If you're successful, I am going to be successful. If you produce, and you get paid, guess what? I am going to get paid too, and again, vice versa.' "

Immediately upon becoming the Panthers' head coach, Fox focused on creating a family environment. Simply put, he wanted to make sure players respected each other—and they liked each other. On the practice field, he wanted the offensive lineman to respect the defensive lineman and vice versa. He repeatedly emphasized that the offense and defense work as one unit, a team. He stressed that his job was to make sure the Panthers organization was a special place to be, and a place where people were proud to come to work. This is what strong leaders do and John Fox did it. In doing so, he was able to turn around a team with a 1-15 record. He made his players believe they could do it and believe in each other. Most important, he made them care for each other.

"John lets the guys know that what he does is for them *and* for his coaches as well as himself to succeed," tells Sunseri. "He's doing it for the whole group. He doesn't individualize coaches or players such as the quarterback or the star linebacker. Everyone has to take a part and do his job for all of us as a collective group to succeed. John includes everyone in the entire organization, from the security guy in the building's lobby to the janitor who cleans our offices at night. He makes everyone feel good about their contribution to the success of the team. He gives credit to everyone—the people who prepare the meals, the people who set the travel schedules, the people who prepare our football fields. 'Everyone must do his or her job, and everyone's job is important.' John makes everyone feel as if he or she makes a significant contribution, and you feel that if you don't do your job, you're letting the team down."

"I evaluate everyone in the organization," Gruden says, "and I want everyone evaluated the same. I want them to know that. I'm talking about everyone from the people that change the lines out there on the field, the people who mow the grass, the people who clean our locker rooms—I want everyone evaluated like the players and coaches. It's all on that scoreboard. When we win, we're happy around here. When we lose, I don't want to see anyone in our building having a helluva day. I can't stand that! When we win, it's okay to smile and be loose. But when we lose, it's a miserable day at One Buccaneers Place. I want everybody to feel it.

"As the head coach, I'm not here to be the social director. I am not here to do anything else but win games. I didn't come here with the idea of forcing myself on anyone. I didn't make any attempt to get to know the secretaries by their first names during my first two weeks on the job. My job was to hire a good staff and hopefully do all we can do to win."

"TO SUCCEED AS A HEAD coach," says Mike Holmgren, "I work at breaking down certain players so I can mold them into accepting a team concept. By nature, the players at this level have gotten to where they are through their individual effort. Their accomplishments are due, in part, to the fact that they had to be a little selfish along the way. Now, to take them to an even higher level, my job is to get them to put their individual fixations on the back burner. Otherwise, there is nowhere else for them to advance. I tell them, 'You are here, at the top of your profession, and now, with better team success, you will garner individual honor.' I am continually working on this concept. It's a tough one to sell, and it's difficult to get them to buy into it. However, when they do, I can show them that really good things happen to every one of them as an individual. If they are willing to accept this, it's the start of a good chemistry base.

"One of the first things that has to be put aside," Holmgren continues, "is the vast differences in salaries paid to players. The guy making millions of dollars can't let the money go to his head. He has to respect his teammates and treat them as equals. The quarterback, for example, must realize that his success relies on the linemen doing their job. The same is true with the running backs and the receivers. In the game of football, every player is dependent upon his teammates. It takes a total team effort. Even though a star player makes considerably more money than an assistant coach or a trainer, he has to listen to the people who are there to improve his performance on the field. Regardless of salary, everyone in the organization makes a valuable contribution to the success of the team.

"I talk a lot about mutual respect," adds Holmgren. "Player to player. Player to coach. I tell them, 'All of us come from different backgrounds. We all listen to different music. We all watch different television programs. But yet we have to live together in a close-knit group for eight months a year. So how do we make this work? We make it work by recognizing that you are different than I am. But, my space is just as important as your space. I am asking you to respect my position. And I'll do the same for you.' This has not been a difficult thing to sell to the players, but it's a message I always deliver at the beginning of every season. Once they grasp it, we get on to the business of football."

Interestingly, Holmgren explains that this speech is necessary because there is a 35 percent turnover of players in today's NFL. "It used to be a lot easier in this League before the high financial rewards and the free agency system," he explains. "Now a player becomes a free agent after five instead of ten years and can play on another team. Today, as the leader my job requires me to seek out new people every year and make sure they blend into the organization."

Holmgren emphasizes that it's not only the players who must have the right mind-set. A winning attitude must permeate the entire organization. Holmgren refers to his seven-year tenure with the Packers: "Many times when I gathered the troops together in the building, and I'm talking about everyone, secretaries and custodians included, I'd point out that for the 25 years following the Lombardi era, there has been a feeling that bad things were going to happen.

'For a quarter of a century, coaches come and coaches go. They change the desks, copy machines, computers. Coaches come, coaches go. Except for you folks, you stayed. And you just watched this happen.

" 'Here's how it's going to be from now on,' I said, 'Whatever I'm feeling on Mondays, you are going to feel.' To implement this, I made a point of visiting these people and letting them know how I felt on Monday. I did this because I believed they should experience the emotions of winning and losing. Everybody in the building had to feel the way I was feeling. That's why, when we won the Vince Lombardi Trophy in '96, I was as happy for the people in the building as I was for the players and myself. After we walked off the field as world champions and were in the locker room together, I wanted to let everyone in the entire organization know how our success was a team effort. I wanted them to be the first people I addressed even before my press conference. I believed the people who contributed to our championship season came first. So with all the media people pounding on the doors to get in, I just let them wait a few minutes so I could talk to the people who were responsible for our victory. And that was everybody in the Packers organization. 'You've all worked very hard,' I said, 'and everyone was on board. I congratulate each of you because what we achieved, we did as a team. You are all champions.' "

THROUGHOUT MY DISCUSSIONS ON TEAMWORK with each of the five head coaches, the word "camaraderie" kept coming up. Mike Sherman talks in detail about how getting the right people in the locker room creates a chemistry that spills over onto the field. "The goal is to get the locker room right," he emphasizes. Sherman thinks the locker room contributes so much to the team's success that when Lambeau Field was renovated, he designed it to promote camaraderie. "Rather than having the traditional long rectangular locker room," he explains, "I made ours the shape of a football. This way, nobody is stuck in a corner. Everyone faces everyone else. All the avenues to different departments—the training room, weight room, equipment room, players' lounge, dining room—have their own artery off the locker room. That's because I believe the locker room is the heart of the football team. It's designed this way to create an environment in which there is interchange among the players.

"When I can create an atmosphere that brings a group of talented men together who truthfully care for each other," he explains, "I assure you they will do well. It's a matter of having the right guys in the locker room on the same page. This is my goal as head coach, and when I can make this happen, we win ball games. I look at winning as a by-product of having chemistry in the locker room, on the team. The goal is the Super Bowl. With the right chemistry among the guys, we are able to handle the ups and downs that the team will face during the NFL season. It is our ability to handle adversity in a game, in a season, that will define us. Sure, the Super Bowl is the goal, but it is also the reward for recognizing and adhering to very specific principles that apply to winning."

"Early in my career, I noticed the fun that the guys have when we're on the road, traveling on planes, and on buses to the airports and stadiums," Sherman continues. "There's a lot of razzing and kidding—it builds a camaraderie that's important for people who have to work together. I suppose the time on buses and planes is fun because there's nowhere for anyone to escape to. And because I saw what happens on buses and planes, my first year in Green Bay I had them get on buses to be transported back and forth to the practice field from the main building at minicamp. Now it's probably no more than 500 yards up or down the hill so they can easily walk, but everybody had to take the bus, players and coaches alike. I wanted them sitting there, hearing Brett Favre and his antics, different players laughing, joking, and acting like kids. It brought them together. It's good for them.

"In my first year here, I was the new guy in town and they didn't know what to expect," Sherman continues. "On the fifth consecutive day of practice on a hot summer day, I had worked the players hard. They were beat, so I figured it was time to have a little fun. In cahoots with two players, Ross Verba and Mike Flanagan, we did a number on the players that they're still talking about. After everyone got on the bus, Verba stood up in the front and shouted, 'The hell with Coach Sherman. The hell with all the damn coaches. We're not going to practice today.'

"There was a sudden hush on the bus. Verba started waving his arms and screaming, 'We are sick of this bullshit. We are not going to do this anymore. We're done with Sherman. We're out of here.'

"Verba turned to the bus driver and shouted, 'Keep on driving. Don't stop at the field.' The driver was in on it and did as he was told. 'Turn right,' Verba ordered him. Go straight. Take us to the bowling alley. We're going bowling.'

"'What the hell are you doing?' Flanagan shouted, grabbing Verba around the neck, acting as if he was trying to restrain him.

"'Are you out of your mind? You're going to get us all in trouble,' a coach screamed.

"When the bus pulled into the parking lot of the bowling alley, I was there waiting for them to let them know it was a day for bowling," Sherman adds. They were in shock that day, and that's what made it work. To pull off a caper like this, I do it when it's least expected. I do it with maybe one or two other guys in on it. Even the coaches don't know what I'm going to do. You have to shock them. I'm always trying to stir the pot so they never know what to expect; therefore they are well prepared for the surprises that life presents to them. It's never the status quo. The message communicated by these antics is powerful."

Jon Gruden concurs. "There is nothing like the team togetherness and camaraderie after a win. It's awesome. It's a rush, a blast. The place where it's most noticeable is in the locker room. I love being around the guys after a big win, the locker room celebrations. And I love flying home with the guys afterward. Every now and then, I'll force a little camaraderie because I feel it promotes teamwork. That's why I'll call off a practice and take everyone to a movie or go bowling. That's why on rookie night the rookies take the veterans out to dinner. To max out and be great, you have to like what you're doing and you've got to genuinely enjoy the people you're with. If you don't, you might be good, but you won't be great."

Just how important is the camaraderie? "It's an intangible that's hard to measure," says Mike Holmgren, "but 20, 30, and 40 years from now, they're going to remember their playing years as the happiest years of their lives. At the Hall of Fame ceremony in August 2003, Hank Stramm was very sick at the time of his induction. Dozens of coaches and players who had worked with Stramm during his 17 years as a professional head coach came to pay tribute to him. These men who came to Canton, Ohio, shared a bond with their teammates that lasts for a lifetime. I've talked to many players whose football careers have long ended, guys like the Joe Montanas and the Steve Youngs who have won every award imaginable, have more money than they could ever spend, and all of these guys will tell you the one thing they miss the most is the camaraderie. The clasping of hands in the huddles—men bonded together with a common goal.

They miss screwing around in the locker room. The practical jokes. The feeling of friendship. The coming together in battle. Yes, it's the camaraderie—something that they never again experience."

WHEN I FIRST STARTED REPRESENTING athletes, I put a small desk and a phone in a small room of my house and I was in business. Today, Lynn and I live in a spacious 4,100-square-foot home that overlooks a canyon in Reno, Nevada. We've allocated space for our business that's separate from our living quarters to accommodate three administrative assistants, plus five computers, fax machines, and other office equipment. We still refer to it as our "home office." We are not a big-time company. We just represent a lot of big-time people. We're a family-run business, and we abide by the same family values that enabled us to build close personal relationships with our clients. If there's one thing I believe separates us from other sports agencies, it's what I call "the Lynn factor." My wife interfaces with all of the coaches and their wives. There are a lot of Bob LaMontes out there, but there is only one Lynn LaMonte.

Each year we develop a management report and present it to each of our clients. The Annual Management Report has ten sections and covers everything from investments to estate planning. It's not limited to business matters. We make a very family-oriented presentation to the coach and his wife and it takes several hours to review. We always present it in person, either at our client's place, or they come to see us. Lynn and I pick them up at the airport when they visit us in Reno and are guests in our home. Sometimes they visit us at our vacation home in Half Moon Bay, just south of San Francisco. They are always welcome to bring their children, and they often do.

Shortly after I started representing professional athletes, I became acutely aware of how short their careers are, especially in the NFL. With an NFL career averaging 3.5 years, I was deeply concerned about what would become of my clients after they could no longer play football. Remember, a majority were still in their 20s. These were young men who have been football players since Pee Wee football and their entire lives evolved around the game. Their diet, weight, school, daily routine, and friends all revolved around sports. From elementary school through high school and college on into the NFL, it consumed them. Consequently, most NFL football players don't have the time to develop other interests. For this reason, a vast majority of professional football players are not easily able to make the transition to ordinary life after football.

Certainly, the star professional player earns a fat paycheck allowing him to be financially secure, but most do not. Seventy-eight percent of all professional athletes two years out of the game are bankrupt, divorced, or unemployed. Even those who are set financially must face the challenge of having a productive life for the next 40-plus years. After all, there is only so much golfing and fishing you can do. There has to be a better way to spend your time or fend off boredom. No wonder so many of them who left the game have posed the question to me, "What am I going to do with the rest of my life?" Incidentally, this question is even asked by those who are financially secure.

It must have been the teacher in me, because I felt a responsibility to provide a program for my clients to prepare them for a successful life transition so they could go on after their NFL days were over. It would be a road map for them to follow for the rest of their lives. I called it, "Invest in Yourself." True, our society conditions us to invest in others because investing in ourselves sounds selfish. But players have to think about their own future during their productive years;

otherwise they won't be able to make the transition when the time comes to leave football and get on with their lives.

And if they don't, they'll end up hurting their loved ones. I won't go into the program in detail, but I will tell you that in 1993 I put together a team of consultants to implement it. Members of my team included Tim Harper, who had been a standout athlete in high school and college with a background in teaching and coaching. His company, Harper and Associates, consulted with people on career planning. Another lifelong friend was Tim Carl, who also taught and coached. Tim has a master's degree from UCLA and founded the Carl Group, a technical writing business. Mike Gough also joined our team. Mike had a strong CPA and stockbroker background. He was a professor at DeAnza College.

Previously, everything that was done for ex–professional athletes was reactive, not proactive. Rehab programs existed but ours would be prehab. Our mission statement read:

> *Invest in Yourself empowers professional athletes to be more successful in their athletic careers; to manage their off-season time, thus nurturing important relationships with their family and friends, as well as improving their self-esteem; and to develop their job and life skills to smooth the transition to "non-playing" lives and careers. We stand for the athlete living a healthy, productive life both during and after his or her athletic career.*

In 1995, the Green Bay Packers became the first franchise in the history of professional sports history to use a program of this type. The Packers organization agreed to pay $6,250 per player to participate in Invest in Yourself. Once Mike Holmgren bought into it—and that was an easy sale—I was able to give a presentation to Bob Harlan, the franchise's president and chief executive officer and the Packers' seven-member executive committee. We introduced it to the players during spring camp and fall camp.

"An interesting thing happened," says Holmgren. "At first, the players were skeptical. They were suspicious because they didn't have to pay a penny for it. They also didn't want the extra work. After a while, they realized that it was truly in their best interest and they became willing participants. In my opinion, Invest in Yourself was one of the best investments the Packers ever made because the players realized that we truly cared about them and their families. It demonstrated that we cared about them in ways other than what they could do on the football field. In return, the franchise benefited because it made them better employees and better players. They were willing to listen to us about things they weren't willing to listen to in the past. They wanted to work harder for us. It was a win-win for everyone."

Between 1995 and 2001, more than 400 players with three different NFL teams had participated in the program. "Initially our players couldn't understand why we were doing it for them," tells Andy Reid, "especially because it had nothing to do with football. They wondered why we were doing it and what was in it for us. In time they realized that we did it because we cared about each of them as a person. Once this became the mind-set, we kept hearing, 'No one has ever cared like this before.' So while it wasn't our reason for having the program, we were paid back in spades because they performed better on and off the football field."

BY NO MEANS DOES GREEN Bay have a monopoly on legacies and devoted fans in the world of sports. Team spirit invokes a strong sense of pride when a player puts on a Yankees pin-striped uniform.

And years after former Notre Dame players have hung up their uniforms, they still get teary-eyed listening to the Fighting Irish fight song. Such fierce loyalty isn't limited to team sports. It exists in many venues; for instance, nobody stands taller than a U.S. Marine!

Pride also exists in the workplace. For decades, IBM employees were exceedingly proud to work for Big Blue. Both Thomas Watson Jr. and his predecessor, Thomas Watson Sr. were cultlike figures to IBMers. Throughout the 1980s, Big Blue ranked at the top of *Fortune's* Most Admired Companies list. Similarly, during the Jack Walsh era, General Electric employees were enamored by their leader. Before the collapse of the dot.com industry, Silicon Valley companies' employees took great pride in their jobs. They were caught up in the excitement of being on the cutting edge of a new industry that promised to alter the course of civilization. They were also caught up in their stock options. Indeed they were team players who worked exceedingly long hours into the night; it was not unusual to find them sleeping on cots at their offices.

Certainly like the Packers, success generates pride in corporate America, but there's more to it than a healthy bottom line. There are scores of highly profitable companies that employ people who take no particular pride in their jobs. There are also once-proud employees who worked at companies that have fallen from grace. There was a time when you could spot an Enron employee by the way he or she walked the streets of Houston—there was a swagger to his or her walk. They were proud to work at Enron. It was a badge of honor to work where the smartest and the best people in Houston were employed. Although the company was still in its infancy, pride had been ingrained in the Enron corporate culture. However, once the deceitfulness of Enron's leaders was disclosed, its employees hung their heads in shame. Likewise, there was a time when Arthur Andersen was considered the world's most prestigious auditing firm. A CPA who made partner was viewed as an esteemed member of his community. Arthur Andersen's faulty auditing practices associated with the collapse of Enron promptly obliterated its employees' sense of pride.

A positive work environment energizes people; conversely, a negative one wears people down. Business leaders who instill a sense of pride in their employees reap the benefits in terms of a highly motivated workforce, reduced turnover of employees, and strong employee *and* customer loyalty. Yes, employees' pride carries over to customers as well as vendors. Clearly, when employees take pride in belonging to a winning team, it is good for the bottom line.

Like a football franchise, there are many ways for a business to instill a sense of pride in its people. Companies that have been around for a long time have a history that makes people feel secure because, unlike Johnny-come-lately companies, their company has roots. Generally, the deeper those roots are, the better. American Express employees, for example, like to let people know their company's humble beginnings trace back to the Pony Express. Employees of Ford Motor Company relish the role that company founder Henry Ford played in American history, and in particular, the automotive industry. Boeing employees delight in knowing they work for a company that has significantly contributed to America's past and present military strength, and in more recent years, the nation's successful satellite program. And like a winning football team, a company with dominant market share makes employees feel they are on a winning team.

People feel good about knowing their employer is charitable. Studies reveal that employees feel the company's giving is their giving too. That's because their work contributed to earnings that made the contributions possible. They also take pride in working for a caring company. A company can care in many ways. First and foremost is how it cares for its customers. Caring companies provide a good value and give excellent service to customers. Conversely, companies that take advantage of their customers shame their employees. Imagine, for instance, working for a manufacturer that made shoddy products and had a reputation for reneging on customer warranties! I know people employed by such firms and when asked where they work, their faces flush with embarrassment. You want your people to hold their heads high—and be proud they're on your team.

A company that sincerely cares for its people is rewarded in kind by employees who care back. How does a company care for employees? By respecting them. By providing a good work environment. By providing above-average fringe benefits. By paying competitive wages. By providing opportunities. Companies that do these things walk the talk! When employees are treated well, they do their best work because they don't want to let their boss down. They want him to succeed because his success is their success too. And remember, people truly want to contribute their fair share. They want to be team players and carry their own weight.

It's no different than a football team where each player has a job to perform or a busted play results. When an employee believes his job contributes and makes a difference to the outcome, he becomes a better team player. Every CEO and senior officer in corporate America can emulate the example of Andy Reid congratulating everyone in the building after a playoff win. When was the last time you saw a CEO walking down the corridor giving high fives after annual revenues went over the top? Or saw a line manager make a big fuss over his team when its productivity had a significant increase? While you don't have a game ball to give away, your appreciation can be expressed in a variety of ways that incidentally won't break the bank. As a token of your gratitude, give away theater tickets, treat an employee and his or her spouse to dinner for two at a fine restaurant, or have a beautiful bouquet of flowers delivered to an employee's house, or for that matter, placed on his or her desk. It's not what you give that matters, it's letting them know they made a contribution, and it's appreciated. People want to know they carried their own weight and their teammates know it. They *need* that pat on the back, that high five.

A good leader develops people who understand that when the team succeeds so does the individual team player. In the world of business, an executive's annual earnings are often tied into the company's earnings with bonuses and stock options. So, much as the NFL star player on a championship team receives a more generous paycheck than does a player of equal talent on a perennially losing team, an executive employed by an industry leader earns considerably more than his counterpart. In fact, in business, it is not unusual for an executive to be compensated with stock options that are based on revenues and earnings, both of which are a reflection of the entire company's performance rather than the individual's performance. Hence, the monetary success of the individual is dependent upon the overall performance of the team.

Doesn't everyone in a large corporation have his or her own box to master? It may not be a three-by-three-foot box of turf (although some cubicles aren't much bigger), but isn't each employee responsible to do his specific job? Like a football team, a company also has specialists who make specific contributions. A company benefits from the synergy that results from everyone working together. To solve a particular problem for a customer, a corporate leader must call on the talents of many team members from different departments. Strong leadership is required to coordinate the talents of many people from different areas of the organization. The entire team effort achieves otherwise unattainable results.

Much like the way John Fox teaches the concept behind each play to his Panther players, when employees in the workforce are cross-trained to understand areas other than their own, their work becomes interchangeable with their coworkers'. By clearly understanding how their jobs support other people's jobs, they are able to make contributions that improve work in other departments. As a bonus, they are also able to pinch-hit for an absent employee in another area. By understanding the big picture, they become better problem solvers, and they have the ability to improvise. These employees are good sources for information and good leaders seek their opinions.

Much as a football team consists of players with diverse backgrounds, the same is true in business. As a melting pot of peoples from around the world, America's diversity is one of our nation's greatest strengths. Similarly, a company with a diversity of employees can draw from a cross section of people with many perspectives, a vast resource for innovation and problem solving.

In his second year with Seattle, Mike Holmgren hired his long-time friend Gil Haskell as offensive coordinator. Haskell had coached running backs and wide receivers at Green Bay from 1992 to 1997. Their friendship goes back to their high school coaching days in San Francisco. Other Green Bay personnel also followed Holmgren to Seattle including wide receivers coach Nolan Cromwell, strength and conditioning coach Kent Johnson, tight ends coach Jim Lind, plus several staff members. The other four head coaches also brought in their "team" of assistants—individuals whom they had relationships with, and whom they trusted.

When Mike Holmgren left Green Bay to become Seattle's head coach, many of his Packer staff followed him. Likewise, a new CEO of a large corporation often brings in his own team, men and women who he knows work well with him. Knowing that there already is a chemistry among his existing team helps launch a strong start.

One common denominator among these five head coaches is that with each of them the word "I" is replaced by the word "we." Signs on walls in locker rooms serve as a constant reminder: "There is no 'I' in TEAM." Study great leaders in any field and you'll observe that "we" is the most important word in their vocabulary. That's because it invites people to take ownership.

Like a successful football team, a good business leader creates camaraderie among his people. Simply put, it's important for people to like the people they work with. A group of coworkers who don't like each other is akin to a dysfunctional family. To have camaraderie, you start by making sure you recruit the right people, those who will adapt to the company culture. How is this accomplished? You do it by devoting the necessary time during the interview process to making sure each job candidate is a good fit with the other people in your organization. This will entail a series of interviews, asking the right questions, and listening patiently to an interviewee's answers. It is indeed a long, tedious process, but it's worth the effort because turnover is costly, and hiring people who are not a good fit is destructive to morale. In the long run, investing the time upfront by carefully scrutinizing job candidates pays big dividends.

Well-planned open-space offices remind me of the openness of a locker room, an environment that promotes closeness while not invading anyone's privacy. I know several top executives who rarely keep the office doors closed; they do it so subordinates feel comfortable paying them a visit. Likewise, a round-shaped conference table that doesn't have anyone seated at the head of the table makes people feel at ease and willing to participate in the meeting. My daughter, Lisa VanDelofske, is a financial analyst at Hewlett Packard, a company with an open-office concept where there are no walls in large areas of its offices. Lisa says that HP does it to remove barriers. It promotes togetherness and better communication.

I believe executive dining rooms, private parking lots, and executive bathrooms should be banned from the workplace. Creating an environment that fosters a "class system" can creates an us-versus-them mind-set in work relationships. Such barriers stifle teamwork. Labor and management shouldn't be pitted at opposite ends and view the other side as an adversary.

Senior managers should mingle with their people in the company cafeteria. These same executives should regularly visit the offices of their subordinates, again to make people feel comfortable. And when they're there, they should observe family photographs, trophies, and other office décor that imparts hints of friendly nonbusiness topics to discuss. For instance, a boss may say, "Where was that photo of you fly-fishing taken?" Or, inquiring about a golf trophy, he might ask, "What's your handicap?" Sure, it's small talk, but it lets someone know you're interested in him or her as a person, not just as an employee.

Good leaders build camaraderie by spending time outside the office in a nonbusiness environment. This can range from taking someone out for lunch or dinner to an elaborate company party given in celebration of a record-breaking year. A game of golf or tennis is also an effective way to get to know your people away from the office. So is a backyard barbeque at your home, a casual night at the bowling alley, an afternoon at a ball game, and so on. I recently read about the camaraderie that exists among soldiers on the battle-field. The article said that a soldier in combat isn't thinking about the

American flag when he risks his life. He's thinking about his buddy next to him in the foxhole.

While nobody is subjected to life-risking tasks in the workplace, people are inspired to do their best work because they don't want to let down their team. This is what good leadership is all about: *motivating people to do their best work.*

6

Facing Adversity

"Never let your head hang down. Never give up and sit down and grieve. Find another way. And don't pray when it rains if you don't pray when the sun shines."

—LEROY "SATCHEL" PAIGE

Jon Gruden's father Jim coached running backs for the Buccaneers from 1972 to 1973 and later served as the franchise's director of player personnel for three years. Jim lost his job with Tampa Bay, and the Grudens moved to Bloomington, Indiana, where he worked as an assistant coach under Lee Corso.

Known for his work habits and inspirational persona, Corso posted big red-and-white steelplate signs with potent messages on the locker room walls to motivate his players. When two of these signs were replaced with new ones, Jim Gruden brought them home for his young, impressionable son. Both signs were promptly hung above Jon's bed. One read: "Luck is when preparation meets with opportunity." The other: "Nothing ever stays the same. You either get better or worse." Every day, his father would ask, "Did you read your signs today, Jon?" Over the years, these messages became acutely ingrained in the boy's brain. On occasion, he still repeats these words to this day.

Through his father's contacts in the athletic department, Jon was a ball boy for the university's basketball team—undoubtedly the most coveted job in the state of Indiana for a Hoosier youngster. Here, Jon had a bird's-eye view of the colorful, intense Bobby Knight, who became his hero. Two years later, Jim Gruden was coaching under Dan Devine at Notre Dame and the Grudens relocated upstate to South Bend. Such is the life of the family of a football coach.

In South Bend, Jon's newest hero was Joe Montana, the team's standout quarterback, who went on to NFL stardom with the '49ers. With large doses of exposure to the Fighting Irish, the young boy became addicted to football, an addiction that he has never kicked. With Montana as his mentor, Jon quarterbacked his high school team in South Bend. Blair Kiel, another Notre Dame quarterback who followed Montana, was a regular guest at the Gruden house. "He had a white Pontiac Firebird," Jon recalls, "and his dad didn't want anything to happen to it on campus so he parked it in our driveway. Every now and then, Blair would make my day by loaning it to me. Blair and some of his buddies sometimes came to my high school games, and boy did that fire me up. As a high school student, it was really cool to hang out with Notre Dame players."

When Gerry Faust came in to replace Dan Devine as the Irish's head coach, he cleaned house, firing many staff members including Jim Gruden. With a young family to support, Jim took a job as a cardboard box salesman in South Bend. A year later, he got another coaching job with the Buccaneers, and the family moved back to Tampa Bay. Meanwhile, Jon had graduated high school as probably one of the most inspired players ever to have played the game of football. Unlike his older brother Jim Jr. who was a high-honor student and went on to medical school, Jon was an average student. "Jim's grades were so off the charts, I couldn't even think about competing with him," Jon tells. "I figured my best chance to be a standout was on the football field, not in the classroom. I didn't shine as a high school quarterback but I thought I could grow a few inches in college, put on some weight, get stronger, and maybe someday have a shot at the NFL." While Jon had high ambitions, he ended up playing three years of college football as a backup quarterback at the University of Dayton, a Division III school.

"When I was in college, my little brother Jay, who was four years younger, was already bigger than I was," tells Gruden. "Although Jay became an outstanding quarterback and went on to star in the Arena Football League, back then, he was just a big lug. The summer of his sophomore year in high school, he'd just lie on the couch eating crackers, drinking soda pop, and watching MTV. And me. I was the backup quarterback at Dayton and determined to be a star, so I spent my summer getting up before sunrise, running, pumping iron, and throwing footballs all day long. And there was Jay, on that couch all day, stuffing his mouth with chips and popcorn. One day, I said, 'I'm going on my mile run up Old Saybrook Avenue, get off your lazy butt and let's race.' He got up reluctantly, put on his running shoes, and said, 'Jon, you know I don't like to run.'

"We were running neck and neck, and I'm getting madder and madder because he was keeping up with me. I'm thinking that he doesn't work out, and any time now he'll quit. 'You're dying, aren't you, Jay,' I egged him. 'There's no way you're going to make it back to the house.' Then with two-tenths of a mile to go, he turns on a burst of speed and beats me by two hundred yards. To rub salt in the wound, he's in our driveway doing that Rocky dance, waving his arms above his head. That's when I realized I'd never be more than a Division III backup. I wasn't fast enough. I wasn't big enough. I wasn't strong enough. I wasn't good enough. As hard as I worked, I wasn't going to get good enough to be a starter. Not even at Dayton, a Division III school. I was devastated. Later that summer, Jay and I got in a fight and he beat me up. Getting beat up by your little brother was the final blow. It was the exclamation point on my athletic career.

"From that point on, I began to think about coaching," adds Gruden. "What else could I do? I loved football and it was my only interest. I said to myself that I better try to get into coaching; otherwise I was going to have a short life in football."

Jon Gruden won the Super Bowl in 2003. He's a big-time winner. But he grew up learning to cope with adversity. He saw his father bounce around from one job to another; it was all part of the life of a football coach. It comes with the territory. Jon had personal ambitions of being a great athlete; he never realized his boyhood dream. Sure, he could have thrown in the towel and picked a career far removed from football. That's what the vast majority of people do when it finally sinks in that he or she will never be a professional athlete, a rock star—a somebody. They put their pipe dreams aside and resign themselves to a life of mediocrity. Most people rationalize and call it "maturity." Jon Gruden, however, refused to abandon his love for football. He simply altered his dream and chose instead to be a football coach. Although his rise to the top of the coaching profession was meteoric, it was no a bed of roses. He paid his dues along the way. He put in his time as a gofer; he endured nights of sleeping in his dilapidated Buick. And although he only requires a few hours of sleep a night, like the rest of us, Jon had his share of sleepless nights.

I DIDN'T GET OUT OF bed one day transformed from a schoolteacher into a sports agent. Like the five coaches in this book, I paid my dues. Like other successful people, I had my share of setbacks along the way. In retrospect, I learned more from the disappointments I suffered than the successes I had. It may sound like a cliché, but I know from personal experience that when we overcome adversity, we become stronger.

To supplement my teaching salary, I taught history during the summer months at both the high school and junior college levels. In 1978, to reduce taxes for homeowners, the State of California passed Proposition 13. With the ensuing loss of tax revenues, the state made massive spending cuts that greatly reduced budgets for schools, libraries, fire and police departments, and so on. Consequently, I lost my summer teaching jobs, and at age 30, with a wife and four children to support, I had to come up with a way to replace this lost income. A realtor suggested that I should sell real estate, and he offered to pay the fee for my real estate classes. Once I got my license, I sold homes on a part-time basis.

After pounding the pavement to drum up sales, I became acutely aware that the world wasn't waiting for Bob LaMonte to sell anyone a home. Before getting my first listing, I had many doors slammed in my face. I quickly discovered that there weren't too many people out there waiting for a novice real estate agent—and a part-time one at that!—to come by and sell their most valuable asset—their home. After soliciting dozens and dozens of homeowners, Rich Campbell, one of the high school kids I taught and coached (that's right, the same quarterback who became my first athlete client), mentioned to me that his family was moving. Shortly afterward, I stopped by the Campbell's residence and said that I had a real estate license and would like to be the listing agent. They were kind enough to give the listing to me.

Several weeks later, I sold the house. It was my very first real estate transaction. My first sale! At a meeting with the buying agent, he handed me a signed contract and a deposit check that the State of California required to be deposited in an escrow account. The jubilation I felt on my way back to my realtor's office is a feeling I'll never forget. I felt like a freshman who just found out he had made the varsity football team; a high school kid who scored his first-ever touchdown. It was a real high. Once I arrived at my office, I called Sharon and Dick Campbell to tell them that their house had been sold. "And we got your full asking price," I said. They were ecstatic. "Thank you so much for the confidence you had in me," I told them.

"It's you, Bob, who should be thanked," they responded.

When I sat down at my desk to review the paperwork, I was beaming and stared at the contract for at least five minutes. Then panic set in. Where was the check? I couldn't find the deposit check! I searched my briefcase and every inch of my car's interior, but still no check. I rushed back to the buyer's agent and told him what had happened. I was mortified. "Have you seen it anywhere?" I asked. "Do you have it?"

"How could you lose the check?" he questioned. "I've never known anyone in my life who lost an escrow check."

"I am so sorry," I apologized, knowing that he had a vested interest in the sale too.

"I'll have to ask them for another check," he said. Evidently, he saw how badly I felt and let me off the hook because he stopped ranting and raving.

Then I had to make that dreaded call to the Campbells and tell them what had happened. Experienced real estate agents told me that the buyers would "certainly cool off and the sale was dead." I kept calling the other agent and he didn't return my calls. Finally, two days later, he called. "Sorry I didn't get back to you sooner, but there was nothing to report because I couldn't get in touch with the buyers," he said. "But good news. I stopped by their house this morning and picked up a replacement check."

The first real estate sale was a humbling experience for me. However, to my dismay, after having one real estate transaction under my belt, I still continued to get rejection—a lot of rejection! That's because I was viewed as a history teacher who sold real estate on the side. People wanted a full-time agent to sell their home—someone who could give them a full day's work, every day—not a teacher who could only show a home in his spare time. Part-time real estate people weren't perceived as professionals—and in fact, most were not. Throughout my first year in real estate sales, I ran into a lot of brick walls, but I had thick skin and I learned not to take it personally when people said no—which most people said to me. With sheer perseverance and tenacity, I hung in there, knowing that if I made enough calls, I would eventually succeed. And I did. By the end of my first year, I sold 13 houses, and after splitting the commissions with my realtor, I took home about $30,000, almost matching my $35,000 teaching salary. My broker was thrilled. I had out-produced 80 percent of his full-time agents.

I continued to sell real estate, even after I represented Rich Campbell, who was drafted in 1981 in the first round by Green Bay for $1.25 million, which included a $500,000 signing bonus. Although Rich Campbell wasn't the number one draft choice in 1981 (he was number six), as the first quarterback picked, he received the richest contract paid to a college player entering the NFL that year. In retrospect, my real estate experience turned out to be a good warm-up for my future sports agency career because, as I quickly found out, disappointments and obstacles prevail in all fields. Being Campbell's agent didn't assure me a one-way ticket to easy street. A year later, Jim McMahon, an All-American from Brigham Young University, was destined to be the number one quarterback in the NFL draft. I met with his old coach, whom I knew at Andrew Hill High School, a sister school to Oak Grove where I taught. The McMahon family formed a committee to interview prospective agents. After the job I had done for Campbell, I thought I had a good shot at being McMahon's agent, particularly because his high school coach submitted my name as a candidate. Instead, the committee chose to go with a major sports agency.

"You did a tremendous job with Campbell," one of the committee members told me. "But we felt that you were like the baseball player who comes into the major leagues and hits a home run his first time at bat. That doesn't mean he'll ever do it again. We're sorry, Bob, but we had to go with someone more established and with a stronger background."

"Don't give up your day job," he might have added.

I had been thinking about the wonderful coup it would be for me to have signed two sensational quarterbacks, and both from the same local area. But it was not in the cards. It didn't help when McMahon signed on with a huge contract. It was a big disappointment. By the comments people were making, I knew they were thinking, "LaMonte had beginner's luck with Campbell, but lightning doesn't strike twice in the same place." And yes, the same thought had entered my mind. Maybe they were right. I'll never be able to repeat the success I had with Rich. I quickly erased all negative thoughts from my mind because from the beginning I believed I would succeed as long as I was true to myself.

Then there was the one I had that got away. A friend of mine from San Jose, California, introduced me to Moises Alou, a baseball player from the Dominican Republic. I represented Alou and he went as a first-round draft pick in professional baseball. His career was blossoming, and then somebody convinced him that he would be better off with another agency. "LaMonte is not a full-time agent, and therefore he doesn't know what he's doing," Moises was told. When he told us this, Lynn and I were deeply hurt because we treated him as if he were a son and we had spent so much time with him. In all the 25 years we have been in business, Moises Alou was the only client we ever lost.

Much like my real estate selling, as a sports agent, I learned to accept rejection as part of the business. The rejection that I think is the most difficult in my business is the rejection I get representing a player who's a free agent. A free agent is a college football player who doesn't get drafted and tries out for an NFL team. Here you have a young man who was a star athlete in every level of competition he's ever participated in from Pee Wee football through college. To his chagrin, however, he doesn't get drafted. As his agent, the team tells me that he's a borderline player, and if he gets released, I'm the one who breaks the news to him. So I get turned down twice—first from the franchise, and then from the player. And guess who he blames? He says that I did a poor job for him. It's my fault. Remember now, up until this point in his life, he has always made the cut. So, I'm getting double rejection—from the team and from him! Consider too that it's significantly harder to sell a free agent than a top draft choice. That's because the player who goes high in the draft is in much demand.

It wasn't only potential clients who didn't take me seriously. Neither did the franchise owners and general managers who met with me to discuss players' contracts. Compared with the big sports agencies with offices around the world that represented hundreds of athletes

ranging from Jimmy Connors to Tiger Woods over the years, I was
that history teacher who moonlights as a sports agent. The large agencies employ a battery of full-time agents, attorneys, accountants, public relations people, and scores of other specialists. When one of their
agents sits down to negotiate with an NFL franchise, his negotiating
team sits across the table from the franchise's negotiating team. When
I am sitting across the table from a team of negotiators, I sit by myself.
During the early stages of my career, they didn't take me seriously. In
their eyes, I was a history teacher or some assistant coach in PE who
threw out the footballs every afternoon. It took years before I had a
track record that dispelled the notion that I was some local yokel who
didn't belong in the big leagues with the big boys. Fortunately, I was
able to represent some big-name clients, which gave me credibility.
These successes also boosted my self-confidence. No matter what resistance I encountered, I always believed that if I stayed true to myself,
I would prevail. Lynn and my forte was the personal touch we provided as a small family business. As a family-operated business, we
formed close relationships with our clients. "We have a local touch
with a global reach," I'd tell people.

It took a while for me to learn, but I eventually figured out that
when people said no, I shouldn't take it personally. I didn't feel
rejected because they weren't rejecting me. They just didn't want to
live in the house I was trying to sell them. In sales, you've got to be
able to separate yourself from the product or service you sell. And
remember, you can't sell them all! Nobody ever does. If a customer
doesn't want to buy my product, I say to myself, "Some people like
vanilla ice cream and some like chocolate ice cream." Do you see
what I mean? It's a matter of taste. If a customer doesn't like your
product (automobile, insurance policy, dining room set, etc.), it
doesn't mean she doesn't like you. Nor does it mean you failed.

On a funny note, I was invited by my daughter Valerie to speak to her fourth-grade class. Well, you know how adults have to be careful about what they say around children because they hear everything. When Valerie stood in front of our class to introduce me, she said, "Today my dad is going to talk to you about his career. He is a free agent." Evidently she had picked up hearing Lynn and I talk about how difficult it was to work with a free agent, and Valerie thought my services were free. I quickly explained to the class that had I been a free agent, we would never make any money. "However, I do represent free agents," I added, "and as their agent, I do get paid."

FOOTBALL IS A TOUGH, PHYSICAL contact sport. It's not for the faint of heart. Think about it. In every play of every football game, players get hit and knocked down. Then they get back up and continue to play. When a team gets badly beaten, it doesn't forfeit the remaining games on its schedule. The coaches and players learn from their mistakes. The team puts together a game plan for the following week and goes on to complete its season. Backup players replace injured starting players. This is football. The nature of the game is to deal with adversity. Harry Truman could have been an NFL head coach talking to his team when he said, "If you can't take the heat, get out of the kitchen."

With offensive lines averaging in excess of 300 pounds per man, and with 240-pound fullbacks and linebackers running 40 meters in under 4.5 seconds, NFL football is indeed a tough physical sport. Some of those huge linemen bench-press 500 to 600 pounds! These guys hit hard. A six-three, 210-pound quarterback is relatively small and fragile compared to a six-five, 300-pound defensive lineman. It takes a lot of guts to stay in the pocket and release a pass at the last moment with split-second precision under the pressure of a full blitz. It's like playing chicken with a charging herd of bison. Still, check the

statistics and you'll discover that the team with the biggest and bad-
dest linemen doesn't automatically go to the Super Bowl. Nor is it
necessarily the team with the strongest and fastest players. It's not
even the team with the most talent. That's because NFL football
demands people of tough mind as well as physical might. When it
comes to winning in the NFL, mental toughness matters. It's a game
where you get knocked down and you get back up. This is Life 101.
When you face adversity, you don't let it defeat you. Success in life is
going from failure to failure without failing. This is the lesson taught
in Pee Wee football and in high school and college football programs.
It's the same lesson taught in the pros. In the NFL, however, when
you get knocked down, you get knocked down a lot harder.

By the time someone has become an NFL head coach, it's a sure
bet that he's faced his share of adversity and has the intestinal forti-
tude to overcome it. Nobody works his way to the top of this profession without getting knocked down and bruised. All five of the head
coaches in this book played football in high school and college—
nobody in the game who has ever been around that long has steered
clear of adversity. It's part of the game. A good example is Mike
Holmgren, who has been around the longest of the five coaches. In
his youth, Mike was one of the nation's most outstanding high
school players, having been named "Prep Athlete of the Year" in 1965
while playing for San Francisco's Lincoln High School. A standout
quarterback who passed for 3,592 yards in his senior year, he was the
most highly recruited player in California that year. The six-five
Holmgren went on to play four years for the University of Southern
California from 1966 through 1969. It was Mike's misfortune that he
was a passing quarterback and Trojans head coach John McKay
favored a running game.

There had been talk that the Trojans were going to adapt to a passing game around their highly touted quarterback, but this didn't happen. A dislocated thumb and sprained ankle sidelined Holmgren. O. J. Simpson, one of the greatest running backs in the history of football, was also on the team, and he too influenced McKay's decision to stay with a running game. Winning the national championship in 1967 for the second time in five years (McKay won a third national title in '72) helped to convince McKay that there was no need to put the ball in the air when his ground game was so domineering. Smaller and quicker Steve Sogge, Toby Page, and Jimmy Jones quarterbacked the team while Holmgren warmed the bench and watched from the sidelines.

Most athletes used to getting the star treatment would have quit the team, and Mike had his opportunity to hang up his helmet when he suffered a shoulder injury during his senior year. But quitting isn't what Mike Holmgren does. He viewed his scholarship as a commitment to the university and he honored it for his four years at USC. "A lot of guys would have become disenchanted and left," says Gary Reynolds, who heads offensive quality control for the Seahawks. "Mike wasn't about to call it quits. So how does he overcome adversity? He finishes it. When a player is down, he challenges him: 'What are you going to do? Take your ball and go home like you did when you were a little kid?' Answering his own question, he says in a booming voice, 'No. You're going to stay and fight. You finish what you start.' Mike's four daughters have been taught to follow the same rule that he applies to his players and himself. 'When you start something, you finish it.'"

Although Holmgren never played enough to earn his letter at USC, he was such a superb athlete, the St. Louis Cardinals drafted him in the eighth round. He went to the camps of both the Cardinals and the New York Jets that year, however, after putting in so much bench time, Mike never made a comeback. He was dropped after one year in the NFL. After receiving a bachelor of science degree at USC, in 1971 he returned to his alma mater, Lincoln High to teach history. The following year, he began teaching and coaching football at Sacred Heart Cathedral in San Francisco which he did for three years. Those first three years in coaching were accompanied by still more adversity. Between 1972 and '74, Sacred Heart had a sickly record of 4 wins and 24 losses. Again, Holmgren could have thrown in the towel and said, "Coaching isn't for me."

Having lost his father as a teenager, Mike became the patriarch of the family at age 16. Holmgren has always been a fighter. A man with great resilience, he has the tenacity to pick himself off the mat, never giving in to defeat. In a world where our failures outnumber successes, a winning attitude is essential. Mike Holmgren is a man who refuses to allow setbacks defeat him.

Andy Reid was a starting tackle and guard at Brigham Young University in 1979–81. During his playing days at BYU, the school was ranked in the top 15 by both the Associated Press and United Press. A strong, competitive player, like the other four coaches, by the end of his senior year, Reid came to terms with the fact that his playing days were over when he was not included in the 1982 NFL draft. Any dreams he might have had of playing on Sunday afternoons were over. He did, however, stay on at BYU, where he got a job with the football team as a graduate assistant, marking an unpretentious launch of his coaching career.

THE DAY ANDY REID WAS scheduled to arrive in Philadelphia to meet with some of the coaches on the offensive unit, an ice storm caused the plane to be rerouted to nearby Baltimore. After hours of delay,

Reid took a train to Philadelphia and arrived after 10:00 that evening. The Eagles' head of security, Butch Buchanico, had been waiting for his new boss, and knowing that Reid was tired and hungry asked him if he'd like to meet some of the coaches who were waiting at the office for his call. "Andy was bushed," Buchanico says, "but he was also hungry and was anxious to meet some of his assistant coaches. So I called my favorite restaurant, Fredrick's, and said to Freddy's mother, 'Jeannie, I've got the new coach and we need a table for six. I know it's late, but can you do this for me?' It was closing time; however, she agreed to stay open to accommodate us.

"When we got there, there was a long table of businessmen who must have been drinking for hours, and they were having a grand time. They were the only customers in the place, and we were seated at a table next to theirs. When they found out that Andy was at our table, they started doing Eagle chants. Then a guy at the other table who owns a lot of car dealerships in town, stood up, half-drunk, and announced, 'I have a toast to make to the new head coach of the Eagles. Welcome to Philadelphia. Boooo!'

" 'Congratulations, Andy,' I said to him. 'You just broke the record. You're our first coach to get booed before you even started.' Andy burst out laughing. He thought it was hysterical. The car dealer was so taken with how Andy reacted that he sent over a bottle of champagne. Andy went over to his table and personally thanked him. He made a lifetime fan that night. That's the way Andy is. Rather than losing his cool, he diffused what could have been an otherwise awkward situation. Now that I know him so well, this is vintage Andy Reid. Instead of getting bent out of shape over a minor thing and making a mountain out of a molehill, he puts things in perspective."

Reid's assistant, Carol Wilson, remembers her boss that first night in town. "Andy is a Mormon and doesn't drink, but he doesn't frown on people who do. He just drinks one Diet Coke after another. After we left the restaurant, we went back to the parking lot and my car was covered with ice. Andy took out his credit card and scraped off my windshield. 'What a fantastic guy,' I kept thinking to myself."

A flight through an ice storm that was rerouted through another city followed by a train ride to the original destination makes for an unpleasant day of travel. Being booed by a table of loud, tipsy businessmen that same night is rubbing salt into the wound. Andy Reid, however, who has dealt with adversity throughout his career, is too big a man to let small, insignificant things disturb him. Watch him on the sidelines during an Eagles game. He doesn't let a missed extra point, an interception, or a fumble upset him. He's been in the game long enough to know that dwelling on a misplay is nonproductive. That's the game of football. You get knocked down and you get back up. You stay calm. You don't sweat the small stuff.

"You can't change during the tough times," emphasizes Reid. "You can't suddenly be a different person or present things to your people a different way. You've got to stay consistent. You must remain strong when adversity comes your way."

Andy Reid is right. Most of us can lead when times are good. Our mettle is tested, however, during times of adversity.

"WHEN I TALK TO MY players," says John Fox, "I frequently talk about adversity. In fact, 'Your Walk in Life' is one of my favorite topics. I spend a lot of time with them talking about what it is to be a man because there is a direct correlation between this subject and being successful as a football player. I don't limit my conversation to football. I expand it because to succeed on the field, they must be strong men off the field. 'Throughout your walk in life,' I emphasize, 'you will have prosperity. You will also have adversity. You must know how to deal with both because how you do will define you as a man. Some guys don't know how to handle prosperity. Believe me, you are never as good as people tell you that you are. And you are never as bad as they tell you that you are. Don't let anyone tell you any of that. You define what you are.'"

Fox stresses that there is much to be learned from adversity. In his first season, the Panthers won their first three games. There was much jubilation in the Carolinas; however, it soon vanished when the Panthers lost their next eight games. Then they went on to win four of their last five games and finished the season with a respectable 7-9 record. Not many teams in the history of the NFL have had a six-game improvement in the win column from one season to the next. When asked about 2002, Fox says, "Preferably, we'd like to win them all. All of us here think we can win them all, but that's only happened once in the history of the National Football League. We had a good season and we learned a lot from the way it started and finished. The players got to experience the difference between winning and losing— and most importantly, learning from the ones we lost."

Mike Sherman concurs with Fox and says, "I think failure is a strong motivational force in this sport. I tell my players that we will have adversity because it's part of the process. It's going to happen. No company has great returns year after year after year. No football team wins every single game. Sure, it hurts when we lose a game, but one game is only one-sixteenth of the season. In this business, we don't have a lot of time to bounce back, so we can't let a loss eat at us and carry over to the next Sunday. We have to let it go and get on to the next game. If we have a defeatist attitude, it would permeate the entire team. As head coach, I must be the one to stand up and say, 'Okay, we can get past this. We lost one of our receivers. We can get past this. Somebody else has to step up. Who's it going to be?' We may lose two games in a row, and the media jumps on it and is writing that the team is weak, the coaches aren't very good, and we can't win the division title or the Super Bowl. We can't allow failure to make us fail. As a team, we look adversity squarely in the eye and we don't back down. Adversity is our glue—it cements us to each other. It brings us together, and it's part of the process. This sounds funny, but I think adversity can be a good thing! Or as I like to say, 'Adversity is good, but I don't want too much of it.' It's a powerful tool in building a football team. It gives us character."

While the game of football is about dealing with setbacks, adversity isn't limited to the playing field. Players and coaches suffer personal setbacks. This is life. And football teams like all organizations have bad things happen that are not related to sports. For instance, during his four years as Oakland Raiders head coach, Jon Gruden anguished over the death of Leon Bender, a six-foot-five, 308-pound defensive lineman. The 1998 second-round draft pick was an epileptic; he died after having a seizure in the bathroom. His death occurred on May 30, 1998, before he fulfilled his lifetime dream of playing in the NFL. The loss of a young, promising man was a personal loss to Gruden and all Raiders. The following year, another personal tragedy happened when wide receivers coach Fred Biletnikoff's 20-year-old daughter Tracey was murdered by a former boyfriend. A Hall of Famer, Biletnikoff had spent most of his playing career with the Raiders. Still another heartbreak occurred the following year when Eric Turner, a defensive back, died at age 31 of intestinal cancer. One of the most popular players on the team, Turner's nickname was "E-Rock" because he was a rock both physically on the football field and mentally and spiritually off the field. Turner was actively involved in the United Way, the Make-A-Wish Foundation, and the Fellowship of Christian Athletes.

The death of three young people, each with a promising future, puts football in perspective; it is only a game.

SOME TIME OR ANOTHER, EVERYONE faces adversity. Successful people learn from their setbacks and with determination, they get stronger. The weak become discouraged and quit. They abandon their dreams and resign themselves to mediocrity. For the most part, it's a fear of failure that stifles their desire to push forward.

In baseball jargon, you've got to keep swinging for the fences. Babe Ruth, the most famous baseball player of all times, held the home run record for most of the 20th century. But did you know the Babe also holds the record for the most strikeouts? The record book lists the Sultan of Swat with 714 homers and 1,330 strikeouts.

In baseball, a star player has a batting average of .300 or better. A superstar bats .350. Ted Williams was the last player to hit over .400. He did it back in 1941 when his batting average was .406. Of the thousands of baseball players who played in the majors during the past 60-plus years, Williams is the only one who averaged four hits in every 10 times at bat for a completed season (walks are excluded). This means that even the great Ted Williams failed to hit safely six out of every 10 times he went to the plate. Even batting an astounding .406, he had more failures than successes at the plate. Still, every time the great Boston Red Sox outfielder went to the plate, he believed he would get a hit. A baseball player must have this self-confidence. When a player starts to think, "The odds are stacked against me, and I only have one chance in three to get a hit," his lack of confidence becomes a self-fulfilling prophecy. That's because self-doubt will cause his palms to sweat, and he'll fidget with his grip. He'll change his batting stance; his concentration on the ball will wane. Sure enough, he'll end up in a slump, knocking his batting average into a tailspin. Great ballplayers refuse to believe that they will fail. They expect to get a hit every time they step up to the plate.

Likewise, a field goal kicker must believe he will put the ball through the uprights every time he's called to duty. Imagine the pressure he faces, knowing that the outcome of the game rests on his 50-yard field goal attempt. There's also a lot of pressure on a basketball player who stands at the foul line. The professional golfer feels it too when he must sink a crucial eight-foot putt. While we might not have a large audience of television viewers watching our performance, we too have times when we are under pressure to execute. And like the professional athlete, we don't always succeed. But it doesn't mean we failed. In a field of 100 professional golfers in a tournament, there is only one winner. This does not mean there are 99 losers. There are golfers who earn prize money in excess of $1 million, who never finish number one in a golf tournament.

Nobody likes to fail, but the true champions in every field understand that it's part of the game. They accept it, regroup, and calculate new and better ways to succeed. High achievers fail many times before they ultimately win. Conversely, people who fail are those who give up too soon. They're branded as failures. Thomas Edison, the greatest inventor of all time, owned 1,093 patents. Nobody else has ever come even close to this number. While inventing the electric light, Edison made 25,000 attempts before he got it right. A reporter once asked him, "Mr. Edison, how did you deal with 25,000 failures?" Edison replied, "I did not fail 25,000 times. I was successful in finding 25,000 ways the light bulb didn't work." Edison had tenacity. He refused to quit. He would not accept defeat.

A Lesson in Persistence

- Failed in business in 1831

- Defeated for legislature in 1832

- Second failure in business in 1833

- Suffered a nervous breakdown in 1836

- Defeated for Speaker in 1838

- Defeated for elector in 1840

- Defeated for congressional nomination in 1843

- Defeated for Congress in 1848

- Defeated for Senate in 1855

- Defeated for vice president in 1856

- Defeated for Senate in 1858

- Elected President of the United States in 1860

In case you haven't figured it out, the man with the above failures refused to give up and became one of America's greatest presidents—Abraham Lincoln. Thank God for his persistence.

Lee Iacocca's autobiography describes how he got fired by Henry Ford, Ford Motor Company's CEO. Iacocca had been the automaker's president for eight years and one day out of a clear blue sky, his boss asked for his resignation. "Why?" a stunned Iacocca asked.

"It's personal," Ford answered, "and I can't tell you more. It's just one of those things."

In tears, Iacocca pleaded to be told why he was being fired, and Ford answered, "Well, sometimes you just don't like somebody."

Devastated, Iacocca vowed not to get mad, but to get even. That's exactly what he did. He looked adversity squarely in the face, picked himself up, and went to work for Chrysler. Later, as CEO of Ford's cross-town competitor, Iacocca engineered one of the most incredible turnarounds in the annals of business. He could have given up and, as Holmgren says, "take his ball and go home." Instead, he opted to fight back. And he came back swinging!

Winston Churchill once delivered a commencement speech at his old prep school. The great British prime minister stood before his audience and said: "Never give in—never, never, never, never, never, in nothing great or small, large or petty, never give in except to convictions of honour and good sense. Never yield to force; never yield to the apparently overwhelming might of the enemy." With those words, he promptly walked off the platform. It's doubtful that anyone in his audience ever forgot his words. In part, due to its brevity. However, Churchill could have spoken for two hours, which he often did, without having had the impact of his two-sentence speech.

Win or lose, head coaches spend hours studying game films so they can learn from their mistakes. They also study films of their opposition, and knowing the competition's strengths and weaknesses, they put together a game plan. Likewise, a good business leader knows his company's strengths and weaknesses. He knows because he too studies reports. And he too goes down into the bowels of the company to learn firsthand what he must know to make important decisions. He gets feedback from people at all levels of his organization. He studies the strengths and weaknesses of his competitors. When the company loses business to a competitor, he finds out why by digging and analyzing. When an account is lost, he doesn't roll over and say, "Oh well, we win some and we lose some." He takes each loss personally and figures out ways to get the business back—and while he's at it, pick up some extra business he didn't previously have!

I mentioned earlier that the average life span of an NFL head coach is 2.5 years, and that the 30 teams in the League during the 1990s had a total of 89 coaches. These numbers make it bone-chillingly clear that a head coach must produce or he's gone. The turnover rate is not a secret, especially among the current NFL's 32 head coaches. Knowing that the odds of a long coaching career are stacked against them, the best of them believe they will be the ones who defy the odds. They accept the challenges they face, believing they will overcome adversity and survive in the fiercely competitive coaching world of professional football.

In the first paragraph of his book *The Road Less Traveled*, author M. Scott Peck states: "Life is difficult," and then goes on to say that once you understand that, it doesn't matter anymore, you expect it to be. The road to success is filled with speed bumps and detours along the way. An NFL head coach knows that unforeseen adversity could strike at any time. In a physical game like football, a serious injury to a key player or players is a real and constant danger. Bad things also happen that are unrelated to the game. Players and members of their families get sick and hurt, and these too adversely affect the team. Keep in mind that 20- to 30-year-old men with a lot of money are exposed to fast cars, alcohol and drugs, and other outside negative influences that are beyond the control of a head coach. Similarly, all companies are subjected to exterior negative factors that can unfavorably impact their employees. People in all fields get sick, hurt, and die. The loss of a key employee can be devastating, both personally and businesswise. And of course there are a host of other exterior events that are beyond the control of a business leader. They run the gamut, including everything from acts of terrorism to the state of the economy. Note, for example, what happened to the travel industry following 9/11.

Scott Peck got it right. Life isn't always easy. This is a fact that we must accept and move beyond it. A sign that I've seen posted in several NFL locker rooms reads: "Tough times don't last. Tough people do." Accept the fact that you will face adversity—you will either overcome it, or it will overcome you.

I'll conclude this chapter with a quote from Theodore Roosevelt:

It is not the critic who counts, not the man who points out how the strong man stumbles or where the doer of deeds could have done them better. The credit belongs to the man who is actually in the arena, whose face is marred by dust and sweat and blood, who strives valiantly, who errs and comes short again and again because there is no effort without error and shortcomings, who knows the great enthusiasm, the great devotions, and spends himself in a worthy cause, who at the best knows in the end the triumph of high achievement, and who at worst, if he fails, at least fails while daring greatly, knowing his place shall never be with those timid and cold souls who know neither victory or defeat.

7

Adapting to Change

"If past history were all there was to the game, the richest people
would be librarians."

—WARREN BUFFETT

During the first 15 years of his life, John Fox's father, a lieutenant commander with the Navy Seals, was stationed at Little Creek Base in Norfolk, Virginia. The commander spent six months of each year in Vietnam, and in her husband's absence, John's mother was the head of the household. "Mom raised my three younger brothers and me," tells John. "A graduate of William and Mary with a business degree in the days when women majored in home economics and education, she was one determined woman. Now, my father, a Navy Seal commander with two Silver Stars, was one tough guy. But she was his equal. My mom was as tough as nails. Consequently, my brothers and I grew up in a very disciplined environment."

With their father being sent back and forth to Vietnam throughout the four boys' formative years, the Fox family was constantly
adapting to change that revolved around orders from the military.
"We never knew when my father was leaving, nor did we know how
long he'd be gone," John explains. "And, of course, there was always
the worry that he might never come home. Being a Navy SEAL lieutenant commander in Vietnam was a very dangerous job. When my
father had to leave, for some reason, the military sent him at 3:00 in
the morning. So without any notice, my father would wake us up in
the middle of the night and we'd load up all of these bags.

"Our household pet was a Navy SEAL dog. Smokey was trained
to sniff out the Vietcong, and stuff like that. One day I went down to
the training center and I saw my nice little dog, packed with gear on
him. He looked like a killer dog. I'm like, 'Hey, is that Smokey?' Being
military brats, our lives evolved around my father's orders, which
were always subject to change.

"I remember one particular time when my father came back
from Vietnam after a six-month tour, and I was driving with him in
the car. We stopped at a traffic light, and I heard my father mumbling
to himself, 'Why am I doing this? I can't believe this light is making
me stop.'

"I was only 11, and at the time I didn't understand why he acted
that way. I've since figured it out. He had been over there in the jungle, and every day he was fighting for his life. Additionally, he was
making life-and-death decisions for his men. Then, he came back to
civilization and he had to do what a traffic light tells him to do. It was
bizarre. A day ago, he was in combat deep in the jungle under the
most fierce, life-threatening conditions, and 24 hours later, a traffic
light is directing him when to stop and go. Talk about having to adapt
to change!"

The contrast of fighting in the jungles of Vietnam and driving down Main Street U.S.A. is analogous to coming from another planet. It's difficult to comprehend how soldiers orientate themselves to civilian life upon their return home. John Fox grew up observing his father make such adjustments for 15 years. In the process, he learned to live with change. In comparison to the kinds of changes that his father had to adapt to, John's may be less drastic, but have nevertheless been life-disrupting. And because of his early experiences with his father, he nonchalantly accepts change as a normal part of life. His ability to embrace change has served him well throughout his career in football.

FOOTBALL IS A SPORT OF constant change. Every play is different. With 22 players in motion with so many variables, no two plays are identical. A head coach must make adjustments throughout the game based on what the opposing team does, who's injured, the score of the game, the time remaining in the game, and so on. A well-coached team follows its game plan but is flexible in making changes. For example, after a play is called in the huddle, a quarterback may call an audible at the line of scrimmage, a decision based on how he reads the defense. Moreover, every season, there is a high turnover of players and coaching staff members, a condition that is based on the average professional football player's career being 3.5 years; so every season brings on a different crop of players. Consider too that player injuries, the free-agent system, and contract disputes also add to the high turnover in the NFL. Thus, there are few certainties; change is constant. No wonder, few teams ever repeat as Super Bowl champions and win back-to-back Vince Lombardi Trophies.

I emphasize that a leader's ability to adapt to change does not conflict with the importance of sticking to a game plan. A good game plan must be flexible and allow for contingencies, indicating what to do "in the event of . . ." For example, a football team with a strong running attack is behind by 10 points with two minutes on the clock and it has no time-outs. Obviously, it's prudent to pass the ball and work the clock. Head coaches make adjustments in their game plan during halftime. These adjustments are based on many variables, including what the other team is doing *and* anticipating what it will do. When asked once about the secret of his ability to anticipate, the great hockey player Wayne Gretzky replied, "I skate to where the puck is going to be, not where it has been."

When Mike Sherman speaks about change, he says that football is a microcosm of the business world. "Only it's accelerated," he adds, "because one season in the NFL is like 20 years of decision-making for a Fortune 500 executive. Everything is compressed in my line of work. I estimate that the decisions I make in a week's time number a year's worth made by my counterpart in corporate America. During an actual game, a head coach is continually making decisions for every play of the game. He's also held accountable for producing immediate results! And correctly or incorrectly, the fans evaluate him based on the team's instantaneous performance. This happens during the game and is repeated on Monday mornings, throughout the week, throughout the season and in between seasons. While CEOs are under the gun to produce, they have considerably more lead time than do those of us who coach in the NFL."

Jon Gruden describes how he views change during the course of a Sunday afternoon game. "Let's say I call a particular play, and then I spot a roadblock telling me it's not going to work. The play has to be changed, so the quarterback calls an audible. We practice long hours to prepare ourselves so we can switch gears on a dime. It's like driving a car. You're going down the street and you read the road signs. You don't just get in your new silver Jaguar and push the pedal down and go 75 miles per hour. You come to a stop sign, and you have to come to a complete stop. Then you put your turn signal on and turn right. You've got to see the signs. The same applies to football. There are signals going on all the time telling you to make adjustments."

Every Sunday is a new game. The way John Fox sees it, when you win a game you have to put it to rest. "The same is true when you lose a game," he explains, "you've got to put it to rest. That's because the next game is coming. It goes back to preparation. Let's clean up what we did. Was it good? Yes. Can we do better? Yes. Was it as good as it should have been? No. We've got to correct this and this. It's always about change in how we prepare ourselves to win the next game. We have to go into every game believing we're going to win. I don't want anyone on this team to have any doubt."

BEGINNING ON DAY ONE, A new head coach in the NFL is expected to start making changes. Keep in mind that he got the job because his predecessor got the boot. Disgruntled fans want things fixed; they're the customers, the ones who determine ticket sales. Team owners don't like drops in ticket sales so they submit to the demands of their customers. Remember, professional football is a business.

While Reid and Fox took over two of the worst teams in recent NFL memory, even playoff teams that don't win championships have exasperated fans and owners. It's not always enough to play in a championship game; there are pressures to win it. And if your team wins the Super Bowl, they're expected to repeat it the following year. Even though only a handful of NFL teams have back-to-back trophies, fans become irritated when their expectations go unanswered. Consequently, the fans demand change, and when your customers demand something new, it's good business to cater to their demands.

It's not only demands from customers that initiate change, internal people are also aware that change is necessary. "I was fortunate to have a couple of things going for me," explains Reid. "First, there were some veteran players who wanted change. They trusted what I was doing. They understood that if they'd keep pursuing my plan and I plugged in some different guys in positions where we were weak, we'd succeed. Second, we had a veteran defense—guys who had been around for a while. It was made clear to them that our offensive unit was very young, but we were making changes that would make it work. They accepted this and, to their credit, they never pointed a finger at the offense for not doing its part to win football games. Although I was criticized by the media and the fans for taking McNabb as our first draft choice, the players were informed that we were building our offense around him, and over time, the offensive unit would put points on the scoreboard."

As I mentioned, although the fans and media didn't know it, the Eagle players understood that Doug Peterson had been brought in from Green Bay to serve as quarterback until rookie Donovan McNabb was ready to start. They were there on the practice field and observed Peterson teaching the West Coast offense to McNabb, his understudy, who was being groomed to be the starting quarterback. Hence, the players knew change was imminent. They were seeing it happen behind closed doors. And they believed in the team's leadership. Andy Reid would transform the Eagles into a strong contender for the championship title.

CHANGE IS SYNONYMOUS WITH RISK-TAKING. Each of the franchise owners took risks when they hired Holmgren, Gruden, Sherman, Reid, and Fox to serve as their head coach. Think about it. It took guts to hire someone to be a head coach of an NFL team who lacked head coaching experience—experience that many people think is a prerequisite for the job. Think about it. You own a very large company. Would you hire an individual with no experience running a large company—or for that matter, a small company? Certainly these franchise owners could have made overtures to a current NFL head coach. Hiring somebody away from another team is as commonplace in professional football as it is in other fields. They could have also sought someone who had been discharged, or for that matter, one of the many available former NFL head coaches anxious to get back into the game. Or they could have hired a big-time college head coach. Just as the NCAA has proved to be a good farm system for NFL players, many head coaches have also come from the college ranks. Understandably, it is always a risk to bring in a new coach to lead a group of people with whom he has no history. But to hire an individual with no head coaching experience whatsoever does indeed push the envelope.

For example, Mike Holmgren was an assistant coach at three different high schools in San Francisco and San Jose from 1972 to 1980 before working as a quarterbacks coach for one year at San Francisco State and four years at BYU. He landed his first NFL job with the '49ers when head coach Bill Walsh hired him as a quarterbacks coach. "I was essentially a high school coach," confesses Holmgren. "Bill didn't have to hire me, and I've thanked him so many times for giving me the chance. I suppose he saw something and was willing to take the risk. In this business, you take risks on a day-to-day basis, and especially in Sunday games when you call plays. This job requires you to make a million decisions, and if you're not willing to let it hang out the window, then you probably shouldn't do it. In this business you're not going to be right all the time, and you're going to get criticized. It gets a little rough sometimes, but that's part of the deal."

As I mentioned earlier, Mike and I go back to when he was a high school history teacher and an assistant coach. He enjoyed his work and was very good at it. "I was comfortable," he says. "I had a little house, was active in my church, my family was growing up, and things were kind of good. Then to leave all that and jump into coaching like I did, well, that was a risk. Today, when I look at my staff, I get to know these men and some of them are risk-takers and some aren't. I have to know that too. The guys like Jon Gruden, Dick Jauron, Steve Mariucci, Marty Mornhinweg, Andy Reid, Ray Rhodes, and Mike Sherman who worked for me and became head coaches were willing to take risks. That's an important part of leadership."

Being an NFL head coach is not for the faint-hearted. Being a risk-taker is part of the job description. "I've always believed in 'no risk, no reward,'" says Mike Sherman. "Now risks have to be calculated. For instance, after the 2001 season ended, we had some receivers that I didn't think were going to be here the following season due to financial situations. As it turned out, all of our starting receivers either left or I didn't re-sign them. I anticipated a lot of criticism and I sure got it. Everyone was saying, 'You can't do that. You can't go into your season without a bench of veteran receivers.'

"I had to make some quick decisions. For example, to move up to get a guy in the draft, I had to give up a second-round pick. And I looked to see what free agents were available. I couldn't get my first choice, but could go after who I thought was the most talented free agent, Terry Glenn. I also knew that his off-field behavior made him a big risk. I met his agent at the Combine in Indianapolis, and he convinced me that I should talk to Terry. I drove from Indianapolis to Cincinnati and had a three-hour conversation with Terry. After talking to him, I took the risk and gave him a one-year contract. Although he's a little injury-prone, he played for us for the entire 2002 season. Glenn ended up catching 49 passes that averaged 13.5

yards and scored five touchdowns. He did a good job for us and there were no off-field problems. Although I was quite satisfied with his performance, I didn't renew his contract because I had several younger receivers with a lot of potential whom we were developing.

"One of those young players was Don Driver who came with us in '99 but saw little action until 2001 when he became one of our top pass catchers off the bench. Driver started only twice in '01, a year when we were loaded with receivers. I moved Driver up in '02, and as a first-year starter, he was sensational, making 70 receptions with nine touchdowns for 1,064 yards. Only two other Packers receivers ever went over 1,000 yards in their first year as a starter, Billy Howton in 1952 and Sterling Sharpe in 1988. Jumping from the top backup to top receiver earned Driver a Pro Bowl spot and the Packers' 'Most Valuable Player' award in '02."

Following the 2002 season, Sherman took still more bold risks when he made several sweeping changes that resulted in replacing his old linebackers with new ones. This too raised a lot of eyebrows. "I cut one linebacker because I felt his production didn't match his salary and he refused to accept a pay cut. We talked about it, and I was brutally honest with him; only he saw things differently so he left. I also cut a veteran linebacker who led the team with tackles for the last two years. Now even though a player is your leading tackler and proficient at his job, it doesn't mean he's the best for the job. And I wanted the best man for the job. In my opinion, having the most tackles is a very discretionary statistic. Because you can lead the team in this department by making tackles 20 yards down the field, or you can do it by making tackles like Ray Lewis does. He makes them in the backfields of your opponent. So there's a difference there. I took some flak from the media on this decision because all they see is that he led the team in tackles. I try not to let the statistics or public opinion cloud my judgment."

At the end of the 2003 season, did the decisions made by Sherman prove to be good ones? After all, the Packers went 12-4 during the regular 2002 season and were 10-6 in 2003, winning the Central Division title both years. Personally, when it comes to change, I have always been of the opinion that it's not important that a decision be right or wrong. What is important is that a decision is made. I don't believe in second-guessing decision making.

A CURRENT SUPER BOWL WINNER knows that his team must make constant changes to improve because his competition won't be idly sitting through the long winter waiting until next season without a thought as to what they must do to be a championship team. To follow up with another Lombardi Trophy, there must be enough improvement that his current team wouldn't be able to compete with next season's team. That's why you'll never hear the coach of the winning Super Bowl team say, "We're the world's champions so next year we won't change a single thing."

Shortly after Green Bay's 35-21 Super Bowl win over New England on January 26, 1997, Mike Holmgren called a meeting of his coaches. "We are going to have a meeting next week," he announced, "and it's going to be about everything we do. How we practice, how we teach, how we meet, how we travel. Everything is on the table, and something is going to change because I don't want it to be the same thing next year. I want you all to come in with your suggestions. You have a week to think about what we can do better. Now we just won the Super Bowl. You can't do it any better. We were the second team ever to lead the League both offensively and defensively. Having said that, it's all on the table. Everyone's suggestions are welcome. I want the players to know that this is a new year. We are not just going to roll through it like we did last year."

Nobody ever accused Mike Holmgren of being complacent. After winning the World Championship, he was a man on the top of his profession, and there he was, acknowledging that he didn't have all the answers. He was welcoming suggestions. Everything was fair game. Every winning coach knows that nothing stays the same. A team either gets better or gets worse. A championship team is on top this year, but to stay there, it must improve. Failure to improve is going backward.

Every Super Bowl championship head coach knows that there are 31 other NFL teams looking over his shoulder for the magical formula that took his team to the top. Each of those competitors will try to copy it or incorporate it into their style of play. While they're at it, they may even take it to the next level, adding a few improvements of their own. The competition pays a lot of money to good people to watch a lot of film so they can figure out ways to beat the current champion. And when your team is at the top of the heap, it's every team's biggest victory of the season when they beat you.

As Jon Gruden puts it, "There are some unbelievable strategists out there, and if you're not careful, they will steal your plays and your players. They will kill you. They will dominate you. You've got to stay on the cutting edge. You've got to work your butt off to get to the top—and work even harder to stay there."

In the highly competitive arena of NFL football, every team is constantly changing. Teams that you beat last time are capable of beating you the next time. After winning Super Bowl XXXVII, Jon Gruden was well aware of how difficult it is to repeat the success two years in a row. "After you win, you've got to have a short-term memory and go back to square one," he says. "You can't rest on the good things and you can't rest on the bad things. I reminded our guys that the last team to repeat Super Bowl rings was the Denver Broncos back in 1997 and '98. 'It doesn't happen very often,' I emphasized. We have a chance to be great. To be a dynasty. We're down in the record books and what we'll have, we will hold onto forever."

A few months later, when the Buccaneers came back for their first practice following the long winter after Super Bowl XXXVII, Gruden kept repeating to them, "It's time to turn the page. I want you guys to get off the circuit. Stop making the appearances, stop the partying, having a good time and showing off your ring. It's been good. We have it. Let's hold onto it. Remember it. But let's go get another one. It's time to defend our title. We want to win every year. If winning once was good, twice is better. We don't want to be a flash in the pan."

At the end of the 2003 season, the Buccaneers did not defend their Super Bowl title. In fact, Tampa Bay finished third in the NFC South's standings with a 7-9 record. The team's poor showing illustrates how difficult it is for a Super Bowl champion to have a repeat performance. Regardless of Tampa Bay's poor showing in 2003, telling his organization that it was time to turn the page was an excellent message. Jon Gruden is an exceptional leader, and most NFL people believe that he will be the recipient of another Super Bowl ring or two before his coaching career is over.

CHANGE IS CONSTANT. IT'S BEEN like this since the beginning of time when God created the universe's stars and planets that are always in a constant state of motion. Every living thing is perpetually changing—

including our own physical beings. Take a drop of water from a pond, place it under a microscope and you'll observe a microcosm of a countess number of infinitesimally small living cells in a state of constant motion. One consistency in this world is change.

For years Dr. Judah Folkman, director of surgical research at Harvard Medical School and a world-renowned cancer researcher posted a sign on the wall of his laboratory that read: "You can teach but you cannot easily unteach." Dr. Folkman explains that the sign served to remind him and his staff that the medical profession is slow at adapting to change. He points out that for years surgeons always did surgery on patients with stomach ulcers. "Even after tested drugs were on the market that stopped the bleeding," Folkman explains, "many surgeons continued to remove ulcers by surgery. Similarly, cancer surgeons performed mastectomies and removed a patient's entire breast, even after lumpectomies that removed only the tumor from the breast proved to be just as effective."

People in all walks of life resist change. Imagine the chaos that would happen if the government suddenly passed a law stating that the metric system would be mandatory in America! We resist change because we get comfortable with the status quo. But like it or not, change will happen. In fact, the *American Heritage Dictionary* has the following new listing: "Retronym: a word or phrase created because an existing term that was once used alone needs to be distinguished from a term referring to a new development or variation." For example, your black-and-white television was, well, your television. But once televised programs were in color, the new sets were color television and the old ones were black-and-white televisions. Before low-cal milk and 2 percent milk, there was no need for the term "whole milk." And before artificial grass on football fields, the natural stuff was just called grass. Now it's "natural turf."

The armed conflict that occurred from 1914 to 1918 was known for decades as "the Great War" and "the War to End All Wars"; once World War II started, it was renamed "World War I." Likewise, for generations, there were no retronyms for words like "whole-wheat flour," "regular coffee," "day baseball," or "propeller airplane." A review of a handful of retronyms illustrates how new ways are all around us, rendering the old ways obsolete.

When Franklin D. Roosevelt took office in March 1933, the nation faced severe economic crisis. Frightened depositors withdrew funds, causing most of the country's banks to close. An estimated 15 million Americans were unemployed. To bring about change, FDR announced "the New Deal," which was opportunistic rather than theoretical in its approach to solving the nation's problems; hence it lacked a consistent economic (philosophy) agenda. It did however provide hope, and this by itself was a much-needed antidote to move the nation forward. FDR used the idiom in reference to what card players might do when everyone is dealt a bad hand—the players ask for a new deal, the deck is shuffled, and the cards are dealt again. FDR kept trying new things, knowing that he must institute change.

At some time in our lives, all of us have put off making a decision that we knew should have been made. Why? We do it to avoid decision-making that involves taking a risk. *We procrastinate out of fear that we may make the wrong decision!* It's safer not to do anything, so we just "sit on it." Sometimes it's an emotional thing. Rationally, we know that straddling the fence is erroneous. For example, upon receiving a negative report on a company, an investor may delay selling his holdings and consequently watch the price of the stock take a nosedive, thereby incurring substantial losses. As the expression goes, "He who hesitates is lost."

During my real estate selling days, I observed people who were

unable to make a buying decision and consequently passed on pur-
chasing what was their "dream home." Although they wanted to
change residences, they didn't want to leave their comfort zone.
Then too, there were those who were afraid to buy because a better
deal might later be available. Unfortunately, after their dream home
was off the market, they regretted their indecisiveness. "My defini-
tion of a good deal," I'd advise them, "is anytime you can get it."

Then there are those people who stick to the same dreary job for
their entire lives because they're afraid a new job won't be as good as
the one they currently have, and ironically it's a job they can't stand!
In my own case, in the 1980s when I announced I was going to represent professional athletes, I'd hear, "Stick to your day job, Bob. You
can't be a sports agent. That's insane." And inevitably someone
would add, "You're a high school history teacher!"

Later, when I proved them wrong, people credited any success I
enjoyed to "sheer luck." It's interesting how the people who never
take risks are the first to call someone else's success luck. I believe
you make your own so-called luck happen by being well prepared.
It's a funny thing, but when you're well prepared, you don't think of
it as risk-taking. That's because you've stacked the deck in your favor.

Landing a position of head coach in the NFL requires many job
changes during the course of one's career. In professional football,
this is acceptable; it's the equivalent to how a CEO works his way up
the ladder within a corporation, sometimes being transferred a
dozen or more times during his career. There was a time when IBM
had a reputation for moving its people to so many different locations
that insiders said IBM was an acronym for "I've Been Moved." At the
same time, recruiters frowned on résumés that indicated a job candidate had a pattern of switching jobs from one employer to another. It
was a sign of instability; to some, it even indicated disloyalty. Too

many job changes was also a sign of failure that carried a stigma branding a candidate as someone who couldn't hold a steady job.

In today's fast-paced world, an executive who has worked for many companies is often viewed as an individual with "a wide range of experience and vast exposure." Such an individual is also someone who embraces change—a take-charge guy. Conversely, an individual who has worked for the same employer for 30 years might be considered a non-risk-taker, someone who is dated and resists change.

An NFL head coach is constantly studying game films, reviewing his team's strengths and weaknesses. It's an ongoing quest for continual improvement. He also reviews game films of the opposition, looking for weaknesses to give his team a competitive advantage. His counterpart in business doesn't have game films to view, but a CEO does have other ways to evaluate his company and the competition. Internally, a business leader can walk the floor, meeting with employees in the factory and at branch offices. He can ask questions, and let employees feel free to speak out, keeping quiet so he can assess answers and suggestions, always making sure to thank them for their input.

Externally, an astute business leader also does his homework in order to gain ground on the competition. He reads available research information on his competitors and he personally tests their products. How is this done? He shops their stores and he uses their products. For example, Red Poling, a former CEO at Ford Motor Company in the mid-1990s, would personally test-ride Ford automobiles by driving different models to and from work—he did the same with non-Ford cars to familiarize himself with the competition's products—their strengths and weaknesses.

Successful CEOs read annual reports and other available financial information released by the competition. Sure, it takes some digging to read through cumbersome reports, but they do it. It's part of their job. Business leaders also attend industry conventions, and here too, they do it in their ongoing pursuit to acquire information about their competition. They want to know why a rival is doing something faster, better, or cheaper. They want to make sure their costs, sales, and profit margins are superior to industry averages. In short, they keep current with what the other guy is doing. This enables them to formulate strategies to implement change to enhance market share. As the cliché goes, "You snooze, you lose."

The tendency to resist change is certainly more prevalent when one does not have enough facts on hand to make a reasonable decision. Being well informed eases the decision-making process. Strong leaders collect the information they need and move forward. Weak leaders collect too much information, thereby stalling the decision-making process. They suffer "paralysis by analysis," a disease that can be fatal to weak business leaders.

In football, there is a tendency to look ahead to next week's "big game" and not get up for this Sunday's weaker opponent. This is when upsets happen. Successful head coaches don't underestimate the competition. Neither do successful business leaders. Oftentimes, it's the competitor that appears to be ready to file for Chapter 11 that businesspeople underestimate. You've got to be careful with this guy because he can be dangerous. A desperate competitor might start making changes, thinking there's nothing to lose. So what does he do? He changes his advertising, lowers his prices, and makes personal calls on customers to give them competitive offers for their business. He also brings in new people with innovative ideas. The lesson here is, don't count a competitor out because he's down. Like a losing NFL team that beats a League leader, so can a desperate competitor do the same to you. Always give credit to your competition for being able to think.

A Princeton student once asked his professor Albert Einstein, "Why are you giving us the identical test as last year's?" The brilliant scientist answered, "Because this year, the answers are different." Einstein's lesson to his student is well taken. In our ever-changing business world, what worked last year doesn't necessarily work this year.

In the world of business, everything is subject to change. In contrast to our life span, the life of a corporation is perpetual, so in theory it continues long after its founder is gone. A corporation's people change for all the obvious reasons—they retire, they die, they get fired, and they get recruited away by other companies. Real estate changes. Old buildings become obsolete and are replaced by new buildings. As a company expands, additional space is required. National headquarters move to better locations as old neighborhoods deteriorate. Companies also move out of town and out of state. Company names change too. Exxon was formerly known as Standard Oil Company. Avon Products was originally called California Perfume Company. Philip Morris Cos. changed its name to Altria Group Inc. and Andersen Consulting became Accenture Ltd. Even a company's product line changes. DuPont was the world's largest manufacturer of gunpowder and America's largest supplier from the War of 1812 through World War I. American Express's roots trace back to the Pony Express. The list goes on and on. Great business leaders are constantly reinventing their companies. The company they manage today won't be able to compete with the company they will manage tomorrow.

They also know that their competition will constantly improve. To catch up with the industry leader, they must make changes that require leapfrog jumps in order to gain a competitive advantage. That's because the competition is a moving target and doesn't remain stationary. Nobody ever said it was easy to succeed in our ultra-competitive business world. It takes exceptional leadership skills—men and women who are capable of switching direction on a dime.

8

Check Your Ego at the Door

"If you take yourself too seriously, no one else will."

—FRANK LAMONTE

t was late February 1983, and the three o'clock bell rung. "School's out," I said half aloud. "Off with my teacher's hat and on with my sports agent's hat." Unlike some of the teachers who required a change of wardrobe to go off to their second job, I wore the same attire. The guys did everything from house painting to carpentry to make a few needed extra dollars. One teacher was an auto mechanic, another was a security guard, and so on. Some of the women sold Mary Kay and Amway products after school. While some of the teachers dressed casually, I wore a suit or sports jacket, and always with a tie. On this particular day, I was wearing a dark blue suit.

Minutes after the school day ended, I was driving down Highway 101 to the Santa Clara Marriott Hotel. At 4:00, I would be meeting with three of the Toronto Blue Jays' top executives. If the negotiations went well, by the end of the day I would have a signed multimillion-dollar contract for my client, Dave Stieb, the team's ace pitcher. Paul Beeston, vice president; Pat Gillick, general manager; and Wayne Morgan, international director of scouting would be on the other side of the table. The Blue Jays wanted me to come to Toronto, but I requested having the meeting locally because my client, Dave Stieb, lived in Morgan Hill, about 20 minutes south of the Marriott.

"This would be convenient for Dave," I told Beeston's secretary, "and like you mentioned, Wayne Morgan also lives in Morgan Hill. It works for me too because I teach high school, making it difficult for me to get away during the school year. If the meeting is in Santa Clara, I'll come down immediately after my last class and be there no later than 4:00. Also, there are daily connecting flights between Toronto and San Jose."

The next day she called back to tell me that Mr. Beeston and Mr. Gillick were booked on a flight from Toronto that arrived in San Jose at 2:00 P.M. "They're staying at the Santa Clara Marriott," she added, "and look forward to seeing you at 4:00 P.M."

"I know the hotel," I replied. "It's the nicest in the area. Thank you for arranging the meeting and have a nice day."

Admittedly, thinking ahead to the negotiations, I had been somewhat apprehensive throughout my classes that day. I shouldn't have been because I represented the Blue Jays' number one pitcher and a favorite with the fans. My concern, however, focused on the poor relationship between Stieb and the team's management, yet neither side was to blame. Dave's previous representation had gotten him into a war with the organization that had been going on ever since his rookie year in 1979. His agent made continual threats to sign him with another team when he became a free agent. That's what caused the bad blood. Stieb was the franchise's superstar, and the Blue Jays' first starting pitcher with a winning record since they became an expansion team. With a 17-14 record and a 3.25 earned run average in 1982, Dave was named the American League Pitcher of the Year by the *Sporting News*. In 1979, he had signed with the Blue Jays as an outfielder, but later became an All-Star pitcher, and at age 24, he was in the prime of his career.

On my drive to Santa Clara, I kept thinking about the one positive thing I had going for me. I had something the other side wanted. This put me in the driver's seat. But then I knew that I'd be meeting with three of the Blue Jays' top executives, who had fought bitterly with Dave's former representation. The previous year Dave had lost his arbitration case and earned $250,000 for the 1982 season. So from past experience, sitting down to negotiate a Stieb contract was not their favorite pastime. The Toronto media had devoted major coverage to the longtime dispute between the franchise and Stieb; hence the pressure was on these men to come home with a signed contract.

Now along comes a new agent representing Stieb—a history teacher who requested the meeting to start in the late afternoon to coordinate it with his classes. This had to have them thinking that I was some local yokel who was clueless on negotiating a major league baseball contract. The last thing they needed was to sit down with a "loose cannon." I kept speculating on what they would be thinking. "Who knows what could happen when you negotiate with an amateur," they must have thought. Of course, I was only anticipating what was going on in their minds because, had our roles been reversed, that's exactly what I would have thought.

From the lobby of the hotel, I called Beeston's room to let him know I was downstairs. "We'll be right down," he said.

Immediately I picked them out from the other guests in the lobby. They looked like a team of distinguished lawyers, each dressed in a dark suit, each carrying a briefcase. After a friendly introduction, Beeston said, "We made arrangements with the hotel manager to use a room off the lobby. It's right over there." The four of us walked toward a hidden alcove in the back, a private area with an open-arch entrance but without door.

There was the usual friendly conversation about how the rain that day was out of character for California weather, but it still beat being in Toronto, Canada, in February. They asked me how I happened to be a high school teacher and a sports agent. I gave them the usual spiel about my career, knowing they were sizing me up, trying to figure out where I was coming from. I knew the routine and I obliged them. Back then, I worked it to my advantage when the other side didn't know me from Adam. I always figured I had an edge because I had done my homework and knew a lot about them. Not wanting to tip my hand, I played the role of a small-town high school history teacher. It was my version of Columbo, the disheveled detective that actor Peter Falk played in the popular 1970s television series by the same name. And like Columbo, on this particular day, I had a raincoat with me to toss over my shoulder.

"Okay, let's talk business," Beeston said, "and let's see what we can do so both sides can walk out of here happy."

"That's right," added Pat Gillick. "It is important to the Blue Jays organization that we do the right thing for all involved. It's counterproductive to have a ballplayer with a chip on his shoulder and has contempt for management."

"I couldn't agree more, gentlemen," I replied. "Now I think we should be looking at this as a team effort. We are not adversaries. We want to do what's fair for everyone. In the long run, it will result in a win-win for everyone. As I see it, we're here today to establish what both sides can agree is a fair market value for the services of my client."

"Well put," Beeston said.

For the next four hours, we talked and talked. Now and then, a waiter from the hotel's coffee shop stopped in to refresh the coffee. Although it was a friendly meeting, the negotiations were going nowhere. This is when Paul Beeston said to me, "There are three of us, Bob, and only one of you. That's unfair because it is difficult for us to talk in front of you about some of the questions you're asking. Here, however, we can't really say anything among ourselves because it wouldn't be polite to ask you to step outside."

"That's fine," I said. "because the way I see it, one of two things has to happen. Either the three of you will go out of this room to talk to each other, or I can go out of the room and talk to myself."

With that, they cracked up. If there was ever a turning point in negotiations, this was definitely it. My remark broke the ice and led to a breakthrough in the negotiations.

"And we thought there may be a problem negotiating with a high school teacher," Gillick remarked with a grin.

"I like this guy," chuckled Beeston.

In all business deals, it always helps to sell yourself to the other party. They liked me and I liked them. Once rapport is established, reasonable people will generally find a way to compromise on the terms of a contract so both parties can walk away satisfied. Stieb's previous agent was arrogant and hoity-toity; Beeston, Gillick, and Morgan were salt-of-the-earth guys. I felt comfortable with who I was—a high school history teacher. I didn't pretend to be some hot-shot agent who wanted to impress everyone with how important and smart he was. And I wasn't there to make unreasonable demands. I was there because I had a job that required me to negotiate the best possible contract for my client. In short, there was a mutual respect, and each side felt comfortable with the other side.

By 10:00, we had agreed to all the terms and they took out a 20-page boilerplate major league contract that I had reviewed earlier in the week. We filled in the blank spots pertaining to salary, time periods, incentives, and other terms that were written by hand in an addendum. I called Stieb and said, "Congratulations, Dave, you've got yourself a six-year, $6 million contract with the Blue Jays. Come on down so you can sign the papers and we'll celebrate."

Meanwhile, Morgan was able to get Alexander's, the hotel's elegant restaurant that closed at 10:00 to serve dinner to us. Dave had eaten hours before, but he did join us in making a toast over a glass of champagne. After the toast, Gillick said, "I'll tell you one thing; I never want to negotiate with a history teacher again!"

Beeston laughed and said, "You know, we accomplished more in four hours with you, Bob, than we did in four years with Dave's previous representation."

The next morning we all flew to Toronto to attend a major media conference at the Sheraton Hotel where the Blue Jays announced the signing of Dave Stieb. It was the biggest media event that the Blue Jays ever had. That evening and the following day, it was all over the news that the fight between Stieb and the franchise was officially over. The media hailed the signing as "the Treaty of Toronto," and Dave Stieb became known as the Six-Million-Dollar Man.

One reporter wrote, "Bob LaMonte was the straw that stirred the drink." I always liked that line because it reminds me of who I am. My client is the star—he's the one in the limelight, not me. As long as I never forget that I am only the stirring straw, my ego will never get the best of me.

★   ★   ★

IN 1982, WHEN MIKE HOLMGREN coached quarterbacks at Brigham Young University, a young ex–Cougars lineman was one of his assistants. That assistant was Andy Reid, a graduate school student working on a master's degree. "We hit it off immediately," Holmgren reminisces. "I liked Andy right away. We thought so much alike— and, in fact, we still do. I told him, 'If I ever get a head coaching job, I want you to join my staff.'"

The fact that Holmgren and Reid took to each other like two peas in a pod is no mystery. Both are salt-of-the-earth guys who don't allow their egos to get in their way. They were a natural fit.

Holmgren was true to his word. Once in Green Bay, one of the first assistant coaches he hired was Andy Reid. Reid's title was: Assistant Tight Ends / Assistant Offensive Line Coach. Four years later, he was named the quarterbacks coach, a job he held for two years before being hired as head coach by the Philadelphia Eagles.

Ever since we taught high school history and coached back in the mid-1970s, Mike and I have remained good friends. In fact, when he joined the '49ers, I was there behind the scenes, advising him on the negotiation of his contract. In those days, coordinators didn't have agents; however, as his friend I worked as his unofficial agent.

When the Packers asked him to come in for an interview in 1992, Mike asked me to represent him. As his agent, I didn't only negotiate his contract, I debriefed him after each interview because if he didn't make a strong first impression, there'd be no contract to negotiate. The interview presentation I developed for Mike has since been continually refined and used for my other clients that were recruited for head coaching positions. I had the good fortune to have Mike Holmgren as my first head coach client because there was so much demand for his services. Representing him was what you'd call a "sure thing." Right from the beginning I knew we'd have a successful conclusion to the interviewing process.

When Holmgren was named head coach at the Packers, I decided to retire from teaching and become a full-time sports agent at the end of the 1992–93 school year. My decision was based on several factors. First, I would have completed 25 years of teaching. Second, our son Brian would graduate high school, making Lynn and me empty-nesters. Third, with Holmgren as my first head coach client, I decided to specialize in representing coaches. By this time, NFL teams had salary caps for the players, but not for coaches. With the kids out of the house, Lynn and I moved to the Reno-Tahoe area in Nevada and have conducted our business from there ever since.

To avoid any potential conflict of interest, Lynn and I stopped representing NFL players and concentrated on coaches and general managers. Little did I know that Holmgren would recruit and develop so many future NFL head coaches during the seven-year period he coached the Packers. Altogether seven of his assistants went on to become head coaches over the next decade. Nobody else in the history of the NFL had ever spun off so many head coaches in such a short period of time.

Marty Mornhinweg is another head coach who has a long history with Holmgren. When Holmgren was an assistant coach at Oak Grove High School in San Jose, California, Marty was the team's all-state quarterback. As a four-year starter at the University of Montana, Marty established 15 passing records. While quarterbacking the 1987 Arena Football League champion Denver Dynamites, a knee injury ended Marty's playing career. Marty worked under Holmgren in Green Bay for two years, 1995–96, as an assistant coach before spending three years as an offensive coordinator/quarterbacks coach with the '49ers. In 2001, at age 38, Mornhinweg was named head coach of the Detroit Lions. After two losing seasons in Detroit, he lost his job and was hired by Andy Reid as a senior assistant head coach with the Eagles.

Gruden, Reid, Sherman, and Mornhinweg came to me because I represented Mike Holmgren. I met them when they coached under Mike. They knew Holmgren was satisfied with my work and he recommended me. "Lynn and Bob will do a lot more than simply negotiate a contract for you," Mike told them. "They have the complete package starting with interviewing for a head coach's job to financial advice."

I have also represented three other NFL head coaches who were not Holmgren "spin-offs." Past clients include Vince Tobin, who was head coach for the Arizona Cardinals from 1996 to 2000; he was recommended by a mutual friend. Another referral came when Bill Devaney, the assistant general manager of the San Diego Chargers told John Fox to call me. Bill thought we'd be good together. It was as simple as that. And in 2003, Jim Mora called to ask me to represent him. He said his decision to choose me was based on my reputation. Being a sports agent is like any business—do a good job and your reputation generates more business.

PROFESSIONAL FOOTBALL IN THE UNITED States is a small industry in which everyone either knows everyone else or knows somebody who knows someone an outsider wants to meet. With the number of players and coaches who move from one franchise to another each year, everyone in the business has a contact with all 32 teams in the League. With all the television coverage and filming of games, there are no big secrets in the League. There are ways to find out what your competition is doing and figure out how to play them. So when players and coaches jump teams, there's not a lot of worry about them giving away confidential information that will put your team at a serious competitive disadvantage. For this reason, head coaches don't lose a lot of sleep over a coach "defecting to the enemy."

Does this mean that coaches don't mind having a top assistant coach leave to join another team? Of course they mind. Nobody likes to lose a good key employee. And in particular, highly competitive NFL head coaches don't. It boils down to this: When you have somebody who is outstanding at his job, it's hard to replace him. And when you lose somebody who jells with the people in your close-knit organization, he's going to be missed.

Holmgren recalls years back when other people gave him a chance and encouraged him in the beginning stages of his career. "I'd be the ultimate hypocrite," he explains, "if I didn't do the same thing. Early on I let my guys know that. I say, 'I would hate to lose you, and I hope you stay. We need you around here. But if you feel an opportunity of a lifetime is within your grasp, I will do everything I can to help you.'"

Mike and I have had many conversations on this subject. He specifically told me about how talented he believed Andy Reid, Jon Gruden, and Mike Sherman were. "These guys are special," he'd tell me again and again. "They will be able to go on to the next level. No question about it. They're very valuable to me, and I'm going to hate to lose any one of them."

"I'm telling you this as your friend," I'd reply, "you're absolutely right about each of them. They will become head coaches in the National Football League. And when that time comes, I know damn well you're not going to be a happy camper."

"I know that, Bob. And they're so good, they won't make any

stops along the way—you're not going to see them taking a head coach's job in college even though none of them has ever had head coach experience. They will go straight through the pipeline and be successful head coaches. I know these guys—they've got the right stuff."

They also had Mike Holmgren, a wonderful mentor. He didn't teach them classroom theory about leadership. He taught them by example. He was a perfect role model. Most important, Holmgren didn't possess the kind of ego that would keep them in check. I have observed that insecure individuals have big egos; consequently, they resist having talented people around them, who, in turn, might outshine them. Likewise, it's their insecurities that induce them to hold people back from advancing. They don't have the self-confidence to believe they could make it own their own.

As an outstanding leader, Mike Holmgren knows how to delegate to his assistants. Again, he is secure with himself, so he gives them lots of room to excel. He gives them plenty of authority and he depends on their performance to produce winning football teams. Thus, his coaches play crucial roles in the overall success of the organization. Each is an important cog in the wheel. Certainly, like any successful leader, he doesn't like to break up a winning combination. Yet, he is very magnanimous when it comes to letting members of his coaching staff move on to another team. "You can't stop a good man from an opportunity," he has said many times. This doesn't mean that Mike has always been happy with me on certain occasions when I represented one of his assistants for a head coach position. It hurts him to let a top positional coach or a coordinator go. Yet Mike is a big enough man to understand that had he been in their shoes, he would have done the same thing when the right opportunity presented itself.

Mike is living proof for the coaches who have worked under him and others in the League that a quarterback coach or a coordinator can advance to a head coach position. He dispelled the notion that previous head coaching experience is mandatory to success at the top job. Today, my job is considerably easier when I talk to franchise owners about whether one of my coordinators is head coach material—and at the time of this writing, I represent 12 NFL coordinators. When someone comments on how this lack of experience might disqualify a client as head coach material, I point out: "Yeah, I heard the same doubts expressed about Gruden, Reid, and Sherman, and you're right—none of them had been a head coach at any level. Nor for that matter was Mike Holmgren. But you are either going to hire him now or someone else will hire him later." This is exactly what I told the Carolina Panthers right before they made an offer to John Fox. The proof of the pudding is in the tasting. Fox took over a team with a 1-15 record, and two years later, the Panthers went to the Super Bowl.

ON SATURDAY NIGHT, JANUARY 19, 2001, the Raiders were playing New England in Foxboro Stadium, giving the Patriots a home team advantage in a playoff game that would determine which team would face the Pittsburgh Steelers in the AFC championship game the following weekend. The real home team advantage was not the stadium packed with biased Patriots fans; it was the weather. The game was played in a blinding snowstorm that worked against the visiting team's players from California, not acclimated to horrific northeastern winter weather. Aired on CBS, the game had a 17.4 rating, the network's highest Saturday prime-time rating in seven years. An audience of 28.4 million television viewers had witnessed the New

England Patriots eat away at a 13-3 lead going into the final quarter, and with seconds remaining on the game clock, a Patriots' touchdown made the score 13-10 in favor of the Raiders.

Then in one of the most controversial plays in recent history of professional football, Patriot quarterback Tom Brady faded back to pass and was stripped of the ball. The Raiders recovered. The referee had ruled a fumble, and it appeared as though the Raiders were on their way to the AFC championship game. With no time-outs, the Patriots' season seemed to have ended. But wait, an instant replay ruled it an incomplete pass and the Patriots still had a faint chance to kick a field goal and put the game into overtime. Millions of Americans who viewed the play and the replays on television believed that Brady had fumbled. However, referee Walt Coleman applied the "tuck rule," meaning that Brady had not completed his throwing motion and had not tucked the ball away with the intention of running. With 27 seconds remaining on the clock, Patriot kicker Adam Vinatieri kicked a 45-yard field goal that barely cleared the goalpost, sending the game into overtime. On the Patriots' first possession in the overtime, Vinatieri kicked a 23-yard field goal to win the game.

Most people who witnessed what had originally been called a fumble were unconvinced that the replay revealed an incomplete pass. Mike Holmgren put it quite simply: "If 100 out of 100 guys in a sports bar say it's a fumble, it's a fumble."

After the game, Jon Gruden was interviewed on network television. The then 37-year-old coach had no apologies for the loss. Instead he humbly said, "In life you usually get what you deserve." He never blamed the referee for what most viewers thought was a terrible call that literally snatched a victory away from the Raiders and abruptly ended their season, thus killing their dreams for a Super Bowl victory. Interestingly, prior to hiring Jon, the Raiders had the worst reputation in the League for shouting at the referees for bad calls. That's not Jon's style. At the time of the game, it was the biggest event of his lifetime, and he never blamed anyone, not once.

Later, Jon and I discussed what he had said on national television. We concurred that many things can happen in a close game to determine the outcome. A ref misses a face mask violation or a personal foul. Or he does see one and your offensive unit has a big play called back, plus a 15-yard penalty. The ball takes a bad bounce. The ref places the ball down on the grass an inch or so short of a first down. There are all kinds of things that can go against you. Jon and I agreed that to be a big-time winner in the NFL, your team has to be so good that even a bad break doesn't determine the outcome of the game. In other words, winning football teams must expect some bad breaks and still win.

Two years later, I was with Jon when Tampa Bay destroyed the Oakland Raiders 48-21 in Super Bowl XXXVII in San Diego on January 26, 2003. This time, at age 39, he had won the biggest prize in the entire world of sports—the Super Bowl, viewed by 138 million Americans and an estimated one billion people in 180 other countries around the world. And what does he say this time? He complimented his players, their former head coach, Tony Dungy, and his former team, the Oakland Raiders. Most interesting was what he didn't say, which was, "In life you usually get what you deserve." He's a class act.

IMAGINE BEING THE HEAD COACH of a team of 20-something-year-old players making millions of dollars and you are the one who commands them to do grueling, fatiguing exercises for hours at a time. Not only do you command them, you insist that they jump on it! You order them: "Run. Now sprint." "Okay, do it again." "Jump when I tell you to jump." Remember, they don't want to do it. In summer training camp when the temperatures hit 90 to 100 degrees, who would? No boss in corporate America demands subordinates to do anything even close to this—and particularly not seven-figure employees, some making several times the boss's salary! Nobody in any other business deals with so many individuals with such enormous egos and matching paychecks. Even when Jack Welch was CEO of General Electric, he didn't have to do that. It is doubtful that he could have done it.

Do you see where I am going with this? There are a lot of egos that must be controlled, and if not handled properly, there are bound to be major clashes between personalities. I'm talking about the kind of clashes that result in conflict. Conflict that devastates morale and destroys team unity! So far, I have only covered the egos of players and coaches and the potential clashes between them. There are also the Titanic-sized egos of the team owners. Remember now, these are extremely wealthy individuals, and they, too, have big egos. It takes a certain kind of super-rich person to want to own a professional sports team, most likely somebody who craves to be in the spotlight. Their egos haven't been sufficiently satisfied by the accumulation of vast wealth. An NFL franchise, however, is just the ticket for an ego trip of a lifetime.

This is an unusual business. In other fields, the top guy—the boss—makes the most money. In the NFL, the head coach is the boss and he has young players in their early 20s who make a lot more than his coaches and even he. In today's society, people are often judged by their paycheck. It's the job of the head coach to make sure his highest-paid players respect their lesser-paid teammates and coaches. For instance, Mike Sherman has a $100 million player, Brett Favre on his team. Favre is quick to credit his teammates for his success. He constantly praises the Packers' offensive line and receivers for the team's success. Favre, a true team leader, is humble and serves as an excellent role model for his teammates. Sherman can count his blessings that his marquee player is an individual of high character as well as a gifted athlete. Favre has never flaunted his paycheck in the faces of his teammates. To him, it's a nonissue.

"I make it very clear to the players at the beginning of each season," explains Sherman, "that the best players are not always the best-paid players. I point out that there are discrepancies, and after I've talked to them, nobody goes around saying, 'I make more than you,' or 'I'm more valuable than you.'"

Like Brett Favre, there are other superstars in the NFL who have remained humble and unspoiled by their fame and wealth. Not only has this made them better team players and more valuable to the franchise, it enhances their longevity in the game. That's because they remain loyal to their strong work ethic that helped make them superstars. The best example I know of such a player is Jerry Rice, who holds the NFL record for the most touchdown catches. Rice has also had 11 successive 1,000-yard seasons, and has gone to the Pro Bowl 10 straight years. In 1995, Rice had a career-high 122 receptions, scored 17 touchdowns, and gained 1,848 yards.

While visiting Mike Holmgren when he was with the '49ers, I watched Jerry Rice at a practice during summer camp. The temperature was 106 degrees and many of the players were having trouble making it back to the huddle after each play. And there was Jerry Rice, who caught a five-yard pass thrown from the one-yard line and he sprinted 95 yards to the end zone. During the workout, all other receivers stopped running after they caught the ball. I was told that during practice sessions Rice runs every ball he catches to the end zone. He's still doing it. This is what makes him football's all-time greatest receiver. No matter that he's already a legend, he hustles today at age 42 with the same vigor he did as a rookie just breaking into the League. Rice refuses to let his success go to his head. He continues to apply the same strong work ethic that made him a superstar. That's Jerry Rice!

Like Favre and Rice, Mike Sherman hasn't allowed his ego to tarnish his success; he continues to do the very things he did to become a head coach. Mike is the consummate overachiever. He will keep working at whatever he's doing until he gets it right. For example, if there were 250 eligible players for the NFL draft, he personally would watch film on every single one of them. Sherman is the head coach now—he plans on staying there by being as conscientious today as he has always been.

Mike Sherman is not a man to bask in his own self-importance. Even as an NFL head coach, he feels uncomfortable riding in a limousine, so much so that he tries to avoid them whenever possible. Although he works long hours, he stops at the dry cleaners and the grocery store on his way home to save his wife Karen from having to make an unnecessary trip. I chuckle when I think about him telling me how he splurged during his first year as head coach. "For the first time in my life, Bob," he said, "I called information and then, for an extra 25 cents, had the operator connect me." "Yeah, live it up," I kidded him. Success can destroy some people. Not guys like Mike Sherman.

AFTER BECOMING HEAD COACH OF the Carolina Panthers, one of the first assistant coaches John Fox hired was Jack Del Rio. Fox gambled with Del Rio when he gave him the job of defensive coordinator prior to the start of the 2002 season. It was only Del Rio's sixth season as an NFL assistant coach. He had spent the previous three years as linebackers coach for the Baltimore Ravens. Del Rio was only 39 years old at the time Fox hired him. He was an 11-year veteran linebacker, beginning his professional career in 1985 as a third-round draft choice picked by the New Orleans Saints. The former Southern California All-American player also played for Kansas City, Dallas, and Minnesota.

The Panthers defensive unit was sensational with Del Rio at the helm. By the end of the 2002 season, it ranked second in the League after a dismal 31st spot in 2001. Much of the success that John Fox enjoyed in his debut year as a head coach has been credited to the Panthers' strong defensive unit. In his first year as a defensive coordinator, Del Rio became a rising star in NFL coaching circles. He was also a hot prospect for a head coach position. On January 17, 2003, nine days before the Super Bowl, the Jacksonville Jaguars announced that Jack Del Rio had been selected as their new head coach, the second in the history of the franchise. At age 40, he was the second youngest head coach in the NFL, just months younger than Jon Gruden.

With Del Rio as Baltimore's linebackers coach from 1999 to 2001, the Ravens finished second in total defense for three consecutive seasons and won the Super Bowl in 2000 when its defense set the NFL 16-game record by allowing only 165 points. "I wanted Jack to be my defensive coordinator, and a lot of teams were after him," says John Fox. "I explained to him, 'You will get an opportunity to be a head coach if you come here. I'll promote it, and I will help you.' I didn't think it would happen a year later like it did.

"It was the first time in the history of this organization that an assistant coach had become a head coach. Although everyone around here was disappointed to see him go, I like to put a positive spin on things. As I told Mr. Richardson, 'He's already gone, so we have to look at it as a good thing.'

" 'A good thing?' he questioned.

" 'Yes. This is the way we have to treat it. A good thing.'

" 'How's that?'

" 'It's an honor, that's how. It's really quite complimentary,' I replied. 'Look at Mike Holmgren and the mileage he's received for having so many of his assistants move on to a head coach position. The way I see it, what we do and what every organization tries to do is locate and develop the best human talent available. It's a difficult job, but not difficult to figure out. This is true in all businesses as well as ours, and I'm not just talking about players. I'm talking about assistant coaches, trainers, everybody. At the end of the day, when you get the best talent available in the market, you will have the opportunity to be more successful than the others. When we're viewed as an organization that helps its people become successful, we'll be able to attract more talent. On the other hand, if we're known as an organization that holds people back, talent will avoid us like the plague.' The team owner concurred, nodding his head indicating his approval."

Yes, it's true that Holmgren has had many of the best positional coaches and coordinators leave to take jobs with other teams, and all were key people who were difficult to replace. On the plus side, it became easier for him to recruit new talent because the word was out that "a job with Holmgren had promise for advancement." An organization that doesn't let go easily eventually develops a reputation for being a dead end for people at the tail end of their career. So while they may hold on to people, there is a high price to pay because down the road recruiting top talent becomes increasingly difficult. I liken it to a college football team that has a star player go early in the NFL draft. While it hurts to lose a standout athlete, it helps when it comes time to recruit the most talented high school seniors for their freshman class. Having said that, Mike Holmgren lost seven generals over a seven-year period, and continued to excel as one of the NFL's premier head coaches. What a remarkable feat; it's something I consider a strong testimony to his exceptional leadership skills.

"I THINK REAL LEADERSHIP IS empowering others," says Mike Sherman, "and then holding them to a higher standard because you gave it to them. I'm always saying to our coaching staff and personnel people, 'I can delegate authority, but I can't delegate responsibility. I am giving you authority and the power to do your job.' This lets them know that I expect more out of them, but at no point am I absolved of my responsibility.

"I have the same message for the players, but they are reluctant to assume bigger roles. That's because this is what they're evaluated on. It's like I recently said to the team: 'I've been leading this team for four years, and now I'm giving it to you guys. I want you guys to step forward because I really want to develop leaders from within. Just how far we go rests on the leadership that comes from you. I want this to be your football team. I've been a leader here for the past few years, but now I want you guys to do it. I want you to have ownership. It's not just me. We have to forget about contracts and salaries for the next several months. We've just got to be one team and the leadership has to come from the locker room—not the general manager's office down to you but from the locker room up to me. I want you to lead. And we will see how that works.'

"People like to complain about leadership," Sherman adds, "but at the same time they don't want to lead—they want to be led. But a good leader is able to get his people to step forth and assume a leadership role."

A modest man, Sherman did not add, so I will, that only a secure man can invite his people to lead. An insecure man with a big ego doesn't want anyone taking a leadership role; he fears it will undermine his position.

I have said many times that Mike Holmgren would make an excellent CEO in corporate America. Perhaps nothing better exemplifies his ability to lead than how he has recruited and developed strong people to assume leadership positions. Imagine a CEO of a major international multibillion-dollar company losing seven senior members of his management team. This is exactly what Holmgren experienced.

What makes him so exceptional? First, he goes after the best talent without concern that somebody in his organization might outshine him. All too often business executives are guilty of passing over talented people because they view them as a threat. Only the strongest leaders say, "I surround myself with people who are smarter than I. They make me look smart." Second, as Holmgren has proved, he wants his people to succeed and he knows when to let go. As much as he hates to lose a key man, he realizes that there is a time when he must bite the bullet. It is not idle words when he says, "You can't keep a good man down."

IT WORKS THE SAME WAY in corporate America. Some companies become known as dead-end places offering no opportunity for advancement, while others are hailed as a stepping-stone for future advancement. Companies that provide internal opportunities for advancement are desirable places to work, and good leaders create opportunities in a variety of ways. First, they provide incentives for managers to promote their subordinates; and second, they aggressively "grow" their companies. Without growth, a company becomes stagnant and its people can advance only when somebody retires, leaves, or dies. Conversely, with growth comes opportunity because new stores, plants, and divisions necessitate more management. As senior people move up the ladder, others within the organization advance in their footsteps.

A healthy sign of good leadership is a company that is able to promote people from within. When management can't fill key positions at the top of the organization from within, it signals that the company has failed to develop its own people. This is a weakness—well-run organizations train their people sufficiently to enable them to move up the corporate ladder. This is what capable management does. Having to seek people externally also hurts morale. Employees think, "No matter how well I perform, it doesn't matter. The company will hire somebody from outside."

A strong leader has a succession plan in place so the company can continue in the event of his untimely demise. A leader with a big ego doesn't have a succession plan because he doesn't think anyone is good enough to replace him. Or equally foolish, he thinks he is invincible and will reign forever. As an example of how important a succession plan is, the United States Army requires every officer to have multiple subordinates ready to take over his or her job. General Electric has an emergency leader-in-waiting should something happen to its CEO. The principle is simple: The fate of the organization is more important than the fate of the leader. If a qualified person isn't able to step in as the result of a catastrophe, the organization will be severely impaired.

A succession plan also serves as an assurance to employees, customers, and vendors that the company will continue under able leadership when its current leader and management team are no longer around. This assurance makes employees feel secure that their future will not be jeopardized should something unexpected happen to the boss. Likewise, customers and vendors are assured that business will go on as usual because they too have a vested interest in a company that they partner with. A supplier, for instance, could suffer irreparable harm if a major customer went under due to the loss of its leader. The same is true for a company that depends on a key supplier for its wares. I have seen cases when companies have gone with a higher bidder because they didn't want to risk depending on a supplier that didn't have a succession plan.

STRONG LEADERSHIP ALWAYS STARTS AT the top of an organization, and a head coach with a big ego is certain to clash with a player who is similarly endowed with a big ego. Conversely, a head coach who manages his own ego sets a positive example for his young players to follow. As their leader, he must also serve as a role model and a mentor.

For the past decade, Mike Holmgren has served as a role model to seven other head coaches who worked under him. His role model was Lavell Edwards, BYU's legendary head coach. "Coach Edwards was one of the most successful coaches ever, and as good as anyone I've ever seen in the way he treated people," tells Holmgren. "He never put on airs with anyone, and was so humble. I had so much admiration for him that I said, 'I want to be like that.' He was a real inspiration to me, and I try to be that way with my players and assistant coaches."

When Mike Holmgren signed his present contract, he became the highest-paid head coach in the history of the game. No matter, he's still the same Mike Holmgren I knew when we worked together as high school teachers. Mike simply refuses to allow his success to go to his head. "As soon as you start believing it's you [not the team], you're headed for a fall," he says. "I know that I hired them [the players, coaches, etc.] but I have good coaches that do a vast majority of the work around here. And without good players, we don't win games. So it gets back to the team concept. Nobody does it by himself. Sure, I'm the head coach so I may be the one that makes the call. Someone has to make the tough decisions. Someone has to be responsible for taking the risk. But it's the whole group that makes it work. As head coach, you really have to understand that. It's not you.

"Do you really know what keeps me in my place so my ego doesn't take over?" he says with a grin. "It's my family. My wife Kathy is the greatest person in the world and I have the most wonderful four daughters, and now two granddaughters. Well, to them, I'm just another dad. Sure, in my world, as a head coach, I can get people to do things. That's what head coaches do. But around them, their classic line is, 'Hey, Dad, I'm not working for you.' Believe me when I tell you that they know how to keep me from getting a swelled head.

"On a more serious note," Holmgren continues, "every time I look around at the other people in this business, I think to myself that there's an awful lot of smart people in this League. That includes a lot of football coaches and some brilliant money people. Sometimes it's a matter of some of us being a little bit more fortunate than others."

After he'd won the Super Bowl on Sunday, January 26, 1997, in New Orleans, I rode back from the Super Dome with Mike to the hotel in a limousine. We're sitting there together, and I said to him, "Here we are two former high school history teachers. In a million years who would have ever thought we'd be in a limo like this after having won the Super Bowl?"

Mike leaned over to me. "You know, Bob, as great as this

moment is," he said, "is it that much different than when we used to get on the bus after we won a championship game in high school?"

That's Mike Holmgren. Here he is at the pinnacle of success in the world of sports. A billion people watched him orchestrate a 35-21 win over the New England Patriots. And he's equating the high from a Super Bowl win, arguably the biggest sports event in the entire world, to the thrill of driving home on the school bus after a big high school win.

Gary Reynolds, now in charge of offensive quality control for the Seattle Seahawks, also worked under Holmgren in Green Bay. He recalls a similar experience with his boss after the same Super Bowl. "After the game, we flew back from New Orleans that night and there was a huge parade in Green Bay to celebrate our victory on Monday. Now on Tuesdays, I'd always accompany Coach Holmgren to his TV show. So on that Tuesday, when we got in his car, I noticed that the backseat of his car was piled high with clothes. 'What are those?' I asked.

" 'I gotta go to the dry cleaner,' he said, 'to drop some clothes off for Kathy and the girls.'

" 'You just won the Super Bowl, Mike! Are you kidding me?' He wasn't kidding. I go, 'Wow.' "

In high school, Holmgren excelled on the gridiron, becoming a high school All-American quarterback, and was sought after by colleges across America. He went from a 3,592-yard passer in high school to a bench warmer at USC. This would have destroyed a boy with an overgrown ego. High school yearbooks are filled with photos of football heroes who never saw their pictures in print again—pathetic grown men who spend the rest of their lives retelling stories of their boyhood glory when they were "somebody." They keep living in the past because their egos prevent them from moving forward and risking failure! Holmgren isn't a man whose ego prevents him from taking risks for fear of failure. He didn't back away from coaching when one of his first high school teams lost 22 consecutive games. Again, it would have been a good time to call it quits but that's not Mike's style. It's what people with big egos do—they must find something else that feeds their ego. They can't deal with failure.

As long as I've known Mike, I've always been impressed with how he places the needs of his people first. Self-absorbed people with big egos don't tend to the little things for other people. Their self-centeredness smothers their desire to serve others. Holmgren, however, knows that when people's morale is up, so is their performance. He understands that serving their needs has priority over attending to his own needs. For example, when some of his African-American players complained that there was no place in predominantly white Green Bay to get a haircut, Mike imported the services of a Milwaukee barber. When they expressed their dissatisfaction with the training-table culinary selections, he procured a soul-food caterer to make biweekly deliveries of meals from Milwaukee. True, these are no big deal but they are thoughtful gestures—the kind of things people do for others when their egos don't get in the way—the kind of things that don't go unnoticed.

AS A FORMER HISTORY TEACHER, I can assure you that the history books are filled with accounts of leaders with big egos who have self-destructed. Simply put, their arrogance was their downfall. This is true in any arena, and in particular in the highly competitive world of business where every strength must be used to an advantage and every weakness must be minimized. In our free enterprise system, people have choices about with whom they do business and for whom they work. Business leaders who fail to check their egos at the door are destined to see customers, vendors, and customers walk out the door.

I have been blessed to represent five head coaches who are exemplary leaders. All come from humble beginnings and have not allowed success to go to their heads. I am privileged and honored to be associated with such fine men. As their agent, I advise them on everything from contract negotiations to financial matters.

Having said this, it has been a two-way street; over the years, I have learned so much from them. I have observed them in action and have been privy to how they motivate their people to perform at peak levels. I am in awe of the respect and loyalty they receive. I am impressed with their ability to take men from diverse backgrounds and lead them to work together as a team.

What each of these five head coaches has done can be emulated in every business. As they have remained humble, a business leader must not allow his ego to cloud his judgment. Such men and women in leadership positions do not inspire others to follow. They will not be respected or trusted, nor will they receive loyalty. Nor will they be liked. Instead, they will be perceived as self-serving individuals who promote their own selfish agendas. It is important to note that people work harder for leaders whom they want to succeed. They do their best work for leaders they care for, whom they admire.

When I negotiated Dave Stieb's contract with the Blue Jays in 1983, my mission was to sell them on certain terms that were most favorable for my client. But first I had to sell them on Bob LaMonte. Once they were sold on me, getting them to agree on the terms of the contract was the easy part. Had I walked into the meeting with a big ego, I am certain I would have encountered resistance that would have jeopardized the negotiating process.

Recall the first thing Jon Gruden did when he became Tampa

Bay's head coach. When he initially met with the players and coaching staff, he praised his predecessor, Tony Dungy, who was popular during his years with the Buccaneers. "I respect the job Tony did," Gruden said. Then he added, "I don't know how I got here, but I am here, and I want you to give me a chance. Give me the opportunity to implement my program here. *I need your help.*" Note that he humbly asked for their help.

When there is a change in management at the top, employees are understandably apprehensive. They don't know what to expect, but they do anticipate change. In the case of Gruden, they might have been expecting a young, cocky person, but his humility quickly dispelled that notion at that first team meeting. Over time, they have since found out that this first impression was indeed the real Jon Gruden. He was the same man whom they saw on national television after Oakland got beat by New England in the 2001 playoff game, the man who said, "We get what we deserve." Today, the Buccaneers know that their young, dynamic head coach is genuine, or as the players say, "the real deal."

There are many people in leadership positions who will not confess to wrongdoings. Again, it's their egos getting in their way. To them being wrong is a sign of weakness—they think admitting a fault or an error compounds the appearance of being weak. "The human element in professional football or, for that matter, any field, will cause mistakes—this is bound to happen," Andy Reid says, "and when it does, you can't hide it under the table. You've got to admit that you messed up." Reid is the first to admit when he is wrong. With Andy Reid, there is no hidden agenda. He expects the same of his people.

People with large-sized egos are most apt to get into trouble when they are successful. "One of the traps in this business," says John Fox, "is the big ego trip that follows success. Most people simply don't know how to deal with prosperity. There have been many great teams in this League that split up because people's egos got in the way. Here, I'm referring not only to players and coaches. I include general managers and owners. There is a slew of people with big heads that a head coach contends with."

The salaries of head coaches have skyrocketed in the past decade; so has the pressure to produce. With a 2.5-year average life span of a head coach, there is no room in the NFL for a head coach with an oversized ego. There is too much talent out there for a franchise to tolerate it. At today's salaries, management wants—and demands—excellence. Those who fail to check their egos at the door are gone; long term, the players, the assistant coaches, the owners, and the fans will grow tired of them. Having said that, the NFL is a business. If bottom line numbers aren't met, the head coach is gone.

ADEPT BUSINESS LEADERS DON'T OFFER excuses when sales and profits are down. They don't blame others for company failures. Conversely, leaders with big egos can't accept the fact that they performed poorly. After a weak quarter or bad year, when did you ever hear a CEO say, "We get what we deserve?" For example, read what the CEOs of national retail stores say when sales and profits are down due to a poor Christmas season. You won't see many of them admit that their marketing efforts were weak or they stocked their stores with the wrong merchandise. They won't announce that their stores were run-down or that their customers received inadequate service—the real reasons why sales were down. It's never the CEO's fault when business is bad. Instead, you'll hear such lame excuses as: "The weather was too warm so consumers weren't in a holiday mood."

"There was too much snow and ice so shoppers couldn't get to our stores." "Thanksgiving was late this year so our Christmas season was shortened." "These are tough economic times." CEOs take note: *You usually get what you deserve.* Hot or cold, the weather is never predictable. And having Thanksgiving come late shouldn't come as a surprise—this is predictable. The weather and the day of the month that Thanksgiving falls on should be factored into doing business. And the economy? Why is it that other retailers had a good Christmas season? They had the same weather, worked by the same calendar, and they too contended with the same economy!

Weak business leaders are quick to point the finger at others. In the retail field, you'll hear CEOs scream, "We bought the wrong inventory for our customer—fire the merchandising manager." "It took too long to get the merchandise from our warehouse to the floor. Fire the vice president of distribution." "Our systems were down. Fire the IT manager." Rarely does the CEO take the hit; there's always a fall guy. To paraphrase Andy Reid, "You can't hide your mistakes under the table. You've got to admit that you messed up." How often do you see CEOs admit that they messed up? Why can't they understand that it takes a strong man to say, "I was wrong." It's the weak man who is unable to admit to error in judgment. False pride is a dangerous thing. Some history experts believe that Richard Nixon would have fared much better had he admitted to making a mistake during the early stages of the Watergate fiasco. Had he done so, the public would have been forgiving, and Nixon would have finished out his second term. Note from Nixon's experience, the longer you wait to admit being wrong, the more damage is done, particularly when it's inevitable that a faux pas will eventually be exposed.

Leaders with humility seek solutions to problems from their people. They listen to what employees say; they respectfully and graciously thank them for their input. Conversely, big egos prevent arrogant leaders from listening. These know-it-alls can't bear being told by subordinates how to improve conditions. They aren't willing to listen because they are too insecure to admit that somebody beneath them might have a solution they were unable to come up with. It is only when business is doing so poorly that they begin to listen to advice. Only when they get beat up and hit over the head enough times do they eat crow. Then they begin to find solutions and, in time, turnarounds occur. Then look at what happens. When times are good again, they revert back to their true form; their arrogance resurfaces. Like business, their personalities are cyclical.

Bosses with truly big egos find themselves surrounded by yesmen because subordinates have been conditioned to tell them what they want to hear. Those who disagree with the boss are ridiculed and silenced. The boss's strong personality is too overbearing for his subordinates to stand up to. They agree with him because they want to avoid confrontation. Consequently, the boss gets no feedback. He hears only what he wants to hear. Employees are unwilling to take risks; creativity and innovation are stifled.

A strong leader must make people feel comfortable voicing disagreement and he must be willing to listen. Not only does he listen, he thanks them for their straightforwardness and encourages them to speak out. This does not imply that he must always have a consensus because there are situations in which a leader must act with conviction and defy the opinion of the majority. I am reminded of a story about Abraham Lincoln and his seven cabinet members. "Each of you has an equal vote," the president told them, "which is a combined total of seven votes. You should remember, however, that I have eight votes." There are times when a strong leader must move forward without a consensus.

People ask, "How does a successful businessman who has built a dynasty become so arrogant? And with such a big ego, how did he ever become so successful?" Oftentimes, when this individual was first starting out, he had humility. Later, success spoiled him. In the early stages of his company, he spent time in the trenches, talking to employees, calling on customers and vendors. Years went by and as his company prospered, he lost touch with his people and customers. His claim that "I built this company and I know my customer" is no longer true; he doesn't know it. Sometimes it happens so gradually over time that he is unaware that he's lost touch. For years he has had a high profile in business circles and the community. He sits on corporate and civic boards—people come to him for advice; they shower him with praise. No wonder he thinks he knows all the answers. Unlike Jerry Rice, who continues to run every pass he catches in practice to the end zone, as the CEO has prospered, he has stopped listening to employees on the assembly line and calling on customers in the field. He no longer practices what contributed to his early successes.

Good leadership provides opportunities for people to grow. A strong leader doesn't keep a subordinate from advancing either internally or externally. Sometimes this means losing a key employee to another organization. But this is a risk one must take in business in order to attract the best people. In the long run, this enhances a company's reputation as an organization that treats people fairly and provides them with opportunity.

My job as a sports agent isn't limited to negotiations and giving financial advice. I also serve as a sounding board to my clients. I never sugarcoat what I say to them. Everyone else tells them what they want to hear, I tell them what they need to hear, and sometimes it's not pleasant. For example, I'll say, "Look, we lost because you called a bad game. We've got to get better." Or I might say, "Man, if we can't run the ball, we're done." What they won't hear from me is,

"You're a great coach. It's not your fault that we lost." Business leaders must surround themselves with people who tell it to them straight—no sugarcoating.

One more bit of advice. Lighten up. Stop taking yourself so seriously. Have some fun. There are times when I've heard a coach say before a big game, "Okay men, let's go out there and have some fun." A common denominator shared by all five coaches featured in this book is that they all have a good sense of humor. Like Andy Reid, successful business leaders sometimes use self-deprecating humor, making themselves the butt of a joke—people with an ego problem are unable to laugh at themselves.

It is true that football is a game, but to the men who play it on Sundays, it's a business. Just the same, allowing yourself to have fun is part of a healthy attitude toward life and is appropriate in every business. Loosen up and have some fun. Let your people have fun; it will make them feel good about themselves. Create an environment that makes people excited about coming to work every day, and where they'll enjoy working so much, they won't keep looking at the clock at the end of the day when it's time to go home. When people feel this way, it will permeate your organization and flow out the door to your customers. Like my dad always said, "If you take yourself too seriously, no one else will."

Afterword

"When placed in command—take charge."

—NORMAN SCHWARZKOPF

Professional football is indeed a brutal sport, but lest we forget, it is a business. Business in our free enterprise system can also be brutal, with companies fighting fiercely for market share. They do it with a vengeance to drive the competition out of business. NFL teams also go all out to dominate the competition, but never with the intent of putting anyone out of business. NFL franchises need competition to stay in business!

To assure the well-being of its 32 franchises, the NFL places limitations on the total sum of money each team can pay its players. In addition to these salary caps, the draft system favors teams with the poorest records, giving them preference in selecting players. In the selection process, the worst team goes first, then the next-to-worst goes second, and so on until the Super Bowl winner picks the 32nd player in the first round of the draft; the next seven rounds follow the same procedure. The League wants parity so the fans don't lose interest. Perennially losing franchises have low attendance; lopsided games result in viewers switching channels in the last quarter. In a business where revenues are based on ticket sales and advertising dollars, equally matched teams that play games decided in the final seconds create the most excitement and generate the highest profits.

When Thomas A. Murphy was CEO and chairman of the board of General Motors in the 1970s and early 1980s, the company's domestic market share was 47 percent. When asked about this, Murphy said, "You can be sure we'll be competing for *every* car sold in this country to be a General Motors product." When he made this statement, Murphy was well aware that antitrust laws prohibited companies from dominating the marketplace, and at the time, GM was the largest company in the world. Referring to these laws, he said, "Many companies in many industries are big, but none were born big. Their size is the consequence of their success. And even if there are only a few large corporations in an industry, that doesn't lessen the competition. You wouldn't say that the finals of an Olympic race are less competitive than the Boston Marathon, even though the Boston Marathon has many more contestants.

"Of course I want to win every car sale," Murphy continued. "It's like a football team coming off a terrible season that would be satisfied at the start of the season to win half its games. Still the head coach is going to go out and try to win every time because games are played one at a time. It's the same way we sell a product. You're not going to get every single customer, but you have to aspire to. You have to go out there with a positive approach, and convince everyone in the organization that, by gosh, the goal is to sell them all."

Our free enterprise system has antimonopoly laws that place restrictions on companies that dominate a particular industry. The concern being that the elimination of competition is not good for the consumer. Similarly, the NFL is set up to prevent franchises with the deepest pockets from dominating the League. The parity works well. Rarely does a Super Bowl winner receive back-to-back Vince Lombardi Trophies. Salary caps and the draft system work well in preventing Super Bowl repeats. Add the turnover of players due to injury, retirement and trades, and the odds increase even more, demonstrating the difficulty of winning two consecutive Super Bowls. With parities in place, the leadership role of the head coach becomes an increasingly significant factor in determining repeat winning seasons and the long-term success of an NFL franchise. In corporate America too, the success of a company rests on strong leadership. An astute investor invests in people, not products, concepts, or bricks and mortar.

In the competitive National Football League, this year's Super Bowl winner is not a redundant slam-dunk to be a repeat performer the following year. In fact, only seven of the 37 winners have won back-to-back Super Bowls. No team has ever won three times in a row. In the past five years, three Super Bowl winners failed to qualify for the playoffs. The Denver Broncos, the last team with repeated Super Bowl wins (1997 and '98), finished last in the '99 season in the AFC West with a 6-10 record. And after destroying the Oakland Raiders 48-21 on January 26, 2003, the world champion Tampa Bay Buccaneers ended the 2003 season with a 7-9 record. Oakland fared even worse, going 4-12 in 2003.

As a consequence, Oakland's head coach, Bill Callahan, lost his job following the 2003 season, a position he's held for only two years. Six other head coaches were also fired, including Dick Jauron of the Chicago Bears. Two years earlier, Jauron with a 13-3 record, had been named NFL Coach of the Year. No matter, he still got the hatchet. Another casualty was Dan Reeves, who was let go by the Atlanta Falcons. Reeves had been named NFL Coach of the Year five previous times (1984, 1989, 1991, 1993, and 1997). Our client, Jim Mora, replaced Reeves in Atlanta. Mora is the son of Jim Mora, a former New Orleans and Indianapolis head coach. At age 42, Mora is one of the youngest NFL head coaches; however, he has been coaching nearly half his life, most recently as the '49ers' defensive coordinator. With a healthy Michael Vick at quarterback, one of the most exciting players in professional football, the Falcons promise to be a strong contender in 2004.

When Bob Shook and I started writing this book just prior to the start of the 2003 season, there was talk that after a convincing Super Bowl victory, the Jon Gruden era with the Buccaneers could be the beginning of an NFL dynasty! If not another championship season, the Buccaneers were certainly destined to be around for the postseason games. Unquestionably, Tampa Bay was the favorite among the five NFL teams whose head coaches I represented. Our other preseason contenders were the Philadelphia Eagles, Seattle Seahawks, and Green Bay Packers. And although the Carolina Panthers had had an impressive 7-9 season in 2002, nobody picked them to make the playoffs, let alone play in the Super Bowl.

As proof of how unpredictable professional football is, four of our coaches' teams made the playoffs, the only exception being the Buccaneers. The Panthers, the long shot of the group, surprised everyone by going to the Super Bowl. In one of the all-time most exciting championship games, the Panthers lost to New England 32-29, when the Patriots' kicker Adam Vinatieri made a 41-yard field goal with four seconds remaining on the clock.

While all of the five head coaches featured in this book are back for the 2004 season, it's not so unusual for last year's winning head coach to find his head on the chopping block one year later. Fickle fans and owners of struggling franchises have little patience with losing head coaches. Likewise in corporate America, shareholders dissatisfied with company leadership are apt to demand a change in management—witness how disgruntled the Walt Disney Company's shareholders recently tried to oust longtime CEO-chairman Michael Eisner as the entertainment company's top dog. While Eisner managed to stay on as CEO, he was forced to relinquish his chairmanship.

In conclusion, leadership qualities like vision, trust, and passion are essential in the business arena as well as on the football field. So must a leader possess superior communication skills, both as an orator *and* a listener. Remember too, teamwork isn't limited to team sports; it's equally applicable in the business world. Only via teamwork is it possible for everyone to perform together as a unit at peak performance. This is what successful head coaches do. This is what successful leaders do in every field.

A common denominator of strong leaders is their ability to meet adversity head-on and not be defeated by setbacks. As they say in boxing parlance, a true champion is the fighter who gets back up after being down for the eight-count and wins the fight. Strong leaders also embrace change. They understand that change is constant. So rather than resisting change, they welcome it, realizing that change presents opportunity.

And finally, real leaders do not allow success to go to their head. As Somerset Maugham wisely wrote:

> *The common idea that success spoils people by making them vain, egotistical and self-complacent is erroneous; on the contrary, it makes them, for the most part, humble, tolerant and kind. Failure makes people bitter and cruel.*